ALCHEMY AND FINNEGANS WAKE

Alchemy and Finnegans Wake

Barbara DiBernard

State University of New York Press
ALBANY

Published by
State University of New York Press, Albany

Printed in the United States of America

For information, address State University of New York Press, State University Plaza, Albany, N.Y., 12246

Library of Congress Cataloging in Publication Data
DiBernard, Barbara, 1948-
Alchemy and Finnegans wake.
Bibliography: p.
Includes index.
1. Joyce, James, 1882-1941. Finnegans wake.
2. Joyce, James, 1882-1941—Knowledge—Occult sciences. 3. Alchemy in literature. I. Title.
PR6019.09F58 823'.9'12 79-22809
ISBN 0-87395-388-6

TO MY PARENTS

Contents

Illustrations

Acknowledgments

I am indebted to many people for their help with this book. A talk by Robert Boyle, S.J., generated some of the basic ideas; the advice and support of Mabel Worthington gave me the courage to continue; and the unfailing energy and counsel of Zack Bowen helped me bring it to its conclusion.

The English Department of SUNY Binghamton sent me on a semester in London at a crucial time in the development of this study; the chance to work at the British Library and to examine the *Finnegans Wake* manuscripts was invaluable. Miriam Leranbaum, whom I miss greatly, introduced me to the British Museum Reading Room; her interest in my work and her sound advice aided me immeasurably.

Thanks to LeeAnn, Peggy, Robin, and Roma for helping with the typing; to Norma, Suzanne, Mary, and my other friends for reading, listening, and understanding; to my parents for supporting me in every possible way, especially by believing in me.

Portions of this book have previously appeared as articles: "Alchemy in *Finnegans Wake*" in the *James Joyce Quarterly*, 14 (1977); "Alchemical Number Symbolism in *Finnegans Wake*" in the *James Joyce Quarterly*, 16 (1979). I wish to thank the editor of *JJQ* for permission to use this material here.

Material from *A Portrait of the Artist as a Young Man* by James Joyce, copyright 1916 by B. W. Heubsch, copyright renewed 1944 by Nora Joyce, is reprinted by permission of Viking Penguin Inc., New York; Jonathan Cape, London; and the Society of Authors as the literary representative of the Estate of James Joyce. Material from *Ulysses* by James Joyce, copyright 1914, 1918 by Margaret Caroline Anderson, copyright renewed 1942, 1946 by Nora Joyce, copyright renewed 1961 by George Joyce and Lucia Joyce, is reprinted by permission of Random House, Inc., New York; The Bodley Head, London; and the Society of Authors as the literary representative of the Estate of James Joyce. Material from *Finnegans Wake* by James Joyce, copyright 1939 by James Joyce, copyright renewed 1967 by George Joyce and Lucia Joyce, is reprinted by permission of Viking Penguin Inc., New York, and the Society of Authors as the literary representative of the Estate of James Joyce. Material from the *Collected Letters of James Joyce,* Vol. I, edited by Stuart Gilbert, copyright 1957 by The Viking Press, Inc., is reprinted by permission of Viking Penguin Inc., New York, and Faber & Faber Ltd., London. Material from the *Finnegans Wake* manuscripts is reprinted by permission of the British Library, London. Material from *The Collected Works of C. G. Jung,* trans. R. F. C. Hull, Bollingen Series XX, Vol. 5: *Symbols of Transformation,* copyright © 1956 by Princeton University Press, excerpts reprinted by permission of Princeton University Press, Princeton, N.J., and Routledge & Kegan Paul Ltd., London. Material from *The Collected Works of C. G. Jung,* trans. R. F. C. Hull, Bollingen Series XX, Vol. 12: *Psychology and Alchemy,* copyright 1953 © 1968 by Princeton University Press, excerpts reprinted by permission of Princeton University Press, Princeton, N.J., and Routledge & Kegan Paul Ltd., London. Material from *The Collected Works of C. G. Jung,* trans. R. F. C. Hull, Bollingen Series XX, Vol. 16: *The Practice of Psychotherapy,* copyright 1954 © 1966 by Princeton University Press, excerpts reprinted by permission of Princeton University Press, Princeton, N.J., and Routledge & Kegan Paul Ltd., London.

List of Texts Used and Abbreviations

P	*A Portrait of the Artist as a Young Man.* N.Y.: Viking Press, 1971.
U	*Ulysses.* N.Y.: Random House, 1961.
Letters I	*Letters of James Joyce.* Vol. I, ed. Stuart Gilbert. N.Y.: Viking Press, 1966.

Page/line numbers for *Finnegans Wake* (N.Y.: Viking Press, 1968) are included in the text without a preceding symbol. For example, 182.30 refers to *Finnegans Wake,* page 182, line 30. Left- and right-hand marginal notes on pages 260-308 are designated by L and R respectively. For example, 299.L1 refers to the first left-hand note on page 299. Footnotes on pages 260-308 are designated F, followed by the number of the note. 290.F3 refers to the third footnote on page 290. Book/chapter numbers in *Finnegans Wake* are given as II.2 (Book II, chapter 2).

Citations to "The Canon's Yeoman's Tale" are to *The Works of Geoffrey Chaucer,* ed. F. N. Robinson, 2nd ed. (Boston: Houghton Mifflin, 1957). Line and page numbers are given in the text following each reference.

Introduction

"Alchemy is *generally understood to have been* that art whose end was the transmutation of the *so-called* base metals into gold by means of an *ill-defined something* called the Philosopher's Stone . . ."[1] (my emphasis). The tentative nature of this statement and the fuzziness of the terms involved point out the difficulties of trying to define alchemy. The Hermetic Art, as it was called, has had a long, complicated history. Not only did the alchemists of different periods disagree with each other about the nature of the art, but so also did those working and writing at the same time. Commentators similarly disagree about the philosophical basis, processes, and goal of alchemy.

Some modern authorities doubt that transmutation was originally the object of alchemy, and speculate that the idea of changing base metals into gold resulted from the superimposition of Greek metaphysics on Egyptian metallurgy in the first centuries of the Christian era.[2] Egyptian metal workers, experts at creating imitation jewelry by making alloys and coloring metals, never claimed they transmuted metals. However, the Greek belief that a primary matter, manifested in the four elements of earth, air, fire, and water, composed all things, became the philosophical basis for the idea of transmutation. Each of these elements, the ancients believed, gave rise to two of the primary properties: earth to dryness and coldness, air to moistness and warmth, fire to dryness and warmth, and water to moistness and coldness. Since these elements were forms of the primary matter, it was believed that one could be transmuted into another. Taking moisture from water would leave the qualities of dryness and coldness, for example, thus converting it into earth. This seemed borne out by experience—boiling water in a glass flask eventually produces a solid, earthy substance. Since these four elements were the constituents of all things, including metals, the alchemists came to believe that one metal could be transmuted into another, or, specifically, that a base metal could be converted into gold. They also believed that all metals were potentially gold and that Nature constantly worked to bring the other metals to this perfect form. The worker in the Hermetic Art, then, merely helped Nature in this process. As the author of *The Golden Tract Concerning the Stone of the Philosophers* explains it:

> Since . . . the substance of the metals is *one,* and common to all, and since this substance is . . . changed by the virtue of its own indwelling sulphur into GOLD, which is the goal of all the metals, and the true intention of Nature—we are obliged to admit, and freely confess that in the mineral kingdom, as well as in the vegetable and animal kingdoms, Nature seeks and demands a gradual attainment of perfection, and a gradual approximation to the highest standard of purity and excellence.[3]

Because of their belief in the unity of matter, some alchemists began their search for the Stone not in metals, but in a black substance which they felt approximated a primal substance on which qualities could be impressed. This, along with the belief that the Stone existed everywhere, in the most common places, led many workers to search for the Stone in the vilest substance possible. Some literal-minded alchemists used practically any substance, including hair, eggs, excrement, and urine, in their experiments. John Read states: ". . . it would be difficult to name any material known to them—whatever its nature, and however rare or repellent it may have been—which was not at some time or other drawn into the ambit of their operations."[4] An alchemist who worked for three-score years without success and who applied to Thomas Norton for help in ascertaining the true ingredients of the search used, among other things, herbs, roots, grass, hair, eggs, urine, antimony, arsenic, wax, and wine.[5]

Other alchemists, though, the precursors of modern chemistry, worked in a way that we would consider more "scientific"; they subjected different metals to various chemicals, acids, salts, and dyes to produce color and other physical changes to make them resemble gold. Color changes, especially, became very important to them; making a metal resemble gold constituted visual proof that a transmutation had occurred. This opened up manifold possibilities for forgery and deceit in alchemy, a theme which Joyce exploits to the fullest in *Finnegans Wake*.

Basically, the alchemical process consisted of "purifying" various substances in order to form the Philosopher's Stone, the goal of the Hermetic Art. Metaphorically, this purification was represented as killing the body of the metal to release its soul and accomplish its rebirth as gold. At its most basic philosophical level, alchemy embodied the reconciliation of opposites; in it such dichotomies as death-rebirth, body-soul, base metal-gold were resolved. This aspect of alchemy also plays a significant part in *Finnegans Wake*.

Alchemical texts contain differing descriptions of the Philosopher's Stone, but most alchemists agree that it is a "medicine" or tincturing agent which, when projected upon other metals, will transform them into gold. In the *Splendor Solis*, which is referred to in *Finnegans Wake*, the author states that his Stone tinged 1500 parts of silver into gold, and that even larger multiplication followed.[6] There are also many mystical descriptions of the Stone which portray it as the perfect union of opposites, the most common and yet the most valuable substance, the elixir which cures all diseases.

The central dictum of the alchemists was "what is below is like that which is above, and what is above is like that which is below." This doctrine, expressed in the *Emerald Tablet* of Hermes, the so-called father of alchemy, posits a belief in the unity of the cosmos, a correspondence or analogy between the physical and spiritual planes. The redemption of base metals into their perfect form of gold, for example, mirrored the redemption of the human soul from its fallen state into a purified spiritual state. This resulted in a dual alchemical tradition. Many alchemists, whether for the love of knowledge or the love of wealth, worked on the physical plane, trying to transmute base metals into gold, but others felt that the process was spiritual only, concerned with the perfection of the soul. Many tracts claim that the true alchemist is pure of heart, has no interest in obtaining material wealth, and will not transmit the sacred knowledge to the unworthy or use it for improper ends. These "spiritual" alchemists derided the "puffers," those short-sighted alchemists mentioned above who missed *all* the spiritual implications of the alchemical texts, taking the instructions absolutely literally. For some workers, however, these levels could not be separated; for them the process operated on both the physical and spiritual planes simultaneously.

Joyce takes up all these aspects of the Hermetic Art, working them into the "proteiform graph" (107.08) of *Finnegans Wake*. Atherton places "the Occultists" among the structural "books at the *Wake*" and acknowledges Joyce's use of alchemy; he concludes, however, that it is "very unlikely that Joyce was deeply read in esoteric lore."[7] I agree. Joyce could have derived the alchemy in *Finnegans Wake* from a few standard translations and histories available at the time. Examinations of the lists of Joyce's books in *The Personal Library of James Joyce* and *The Consciousness of James Joyce* do not reveal any specific sources for the use of alchemical allusions in *Finnegans Wake,*[8] but the *Wake* does contain allusions to *The Hermetic Museum,* published in London in 1893. This was an English translation of a collection of alchemical texts originally published in Latin at Frankfurt in 1678; the editor, Arthur Edward Waite, calls it "a representative collection of the more brief and less ancient alchemical writers."[9] The articles on "Alchemy," "Hermes Trismegistus," "Thoth," and "Paracelsus" in the eleventh edition of the *Encyclopedia Britannica,* which we know Joyce consulted, also contain much of the information on alchemical theory and practice referred to in *Finnegans Wake.* In this study, I have tried to confine myself to references from these texts and others that Joyce may have used or known whenever possible. Certainly alchemy and the occult were topics generating much interest in the years before and during Joyce's composition of the *Wake.*

The occult revival of the nineteenth century renewed interest in such works as *Theatrum Chemicum Britannicum,* a collection of texts by English alchemists compiled by Elias Ashmole and first published in 1652, and made many previously unavailable texts available. From 1885 to 1906, the French scholar Berthelot, referred to in the article on alchemy in the eleventh *Encyclopedia Britannica,* published translations and studies of many alchemical manuscripts which had lain ignored in various libraries for centuries. The British Library catalogue contains six pages of entries for A. E. Waite, the editor of *The Hermetic Museum*; from 1890–1926 he edited and translated works by such alchemists as Basilius Valentinus, Paracelsus, Edward Kelly, Janus Lacinius, and Raymond

Lully, and wrote books on Freemasonry, mysticism, the Cabala, and the Rosicrucians. During this time also a London publishing house, William Rider and Son, put out a "Mystics and Occultists" series. H. Stanley Redgrove published *Alchemy: Ancient and Modern* (1911), *Bygone Beliefs: Being a Series of Excursions in the Byways of Thought* (1920), and works on occult theory, Roger Bacon, and Joannes Baptista van Helmont under the Rider and Son imprint. In 1912, Redgrove and others founded the Alchemical Society to do justice to the alchemists, whom they felt had been misunderstood.

Stuart Gilbert reports that he and Joyce discussed Éliphas Lévi's theories of magic.[10] Tindall refers to Lévi as "the most eminent magus of the nineteenth century." In his works, Lévi draws on any source which supports his theory that there is an occult doctrine "which is everywhere the same and everywhere carefully concealed. Occult philosophy seems to have been the nurse or god-mother of all intellectual forces. . . ."[11] The works of Lévi were largely responsible for introducing the Hermetic tradition to the poets of the nineteenth century. Joyce, no true believer in the occult, but aware of theories that could be useful to him, refers to Lévi in *Finnegans Wake* ("*Great is Eliphas Magistrodontos*" 244.35) in the context of a zoo which also includes the mystic Jacob Boehme ("behemuth" 244.36).

The modern revivalists of the occult exalted Hermes, Paracelsus, and others for their metaphysics, a view which set forth the integral connection between macrocosm and microcosm, the place of value in the material world, and the inseparability of subject and object. Many of those who turned to alchemy and other aspects of the occult in the nineteenth century desired to return to such a world. However, the occult revival which served as a source of Joyce's knowledge of these things did not really represent the original tradition. Hermeticism had gone underground in the Middle Ages, and when it reappeared, it was with a difference. The Renaissance alchemists such as Cornelius Agrippa and Jacob Boehme, Cixous says, "were more theologians than magi." She continues:

> In fact, the Hermeticism which was known to Joyce had undergone many changes and been bastardised by the addition of much alchemical material, theology derived from Meister Eckhart, and simple magic during the nineteenth century.[12]

Infused by magic, theology, spiritualism, and the desire for an interrelated cosmos, the alchemy with which Joyce would have been familiar favored the spiritual over the physical. Redgrove attempts to reconcile the two views, but, by suggesting that physical alchemy was primarily a method for proving a world view, he still shows his preference for the spiritual interpretation. In his words:

> Alchemy was both a philosophy and an experimental science, and the transmutation of the metals was its end only in that this would give the final proof of the alchemistic hypotheses; in other words, Alchemy, considered from the physical standpoint, was the attempt to demonstrate experimentally on the material plane the validity of a certain philosophical view of the Cosmos.[13]

Joyce uses alchemy, especially in *Finnegans Wake,* as a metaphor for change and the artistic process; the alchemical transmutation of lead into gold parallels the artistic transmutation of life into art. However, Joyce's references to alchemy show that he rejects both the purely spiritual and the purely physical explanations of the Hermetic Art. The "spiritual" alchemists wanted nothing at all to do with chemicals, furnaces, or laboratory processes; they wanted to transcend the physical. On the other hand, the literal-minded alchemists, who combined the most vile substances to form the Stone, remained mired in the physical, unaware that the texts and processes could be interpreted on another level. Joyce's view of the artist/alchemist harmonizes these two views. The artist, Joyce suggests in all his works, but most strongly in *Finnegans Wake,* uses the elements of the messy, chaotic, fragmented everyday world to create an art which transforms but does not lose sight of its origins. *Finnegans Wake* never allows the reader to fly freely above the world like Dedalus; like the fallen Icarus, the reader, plunged into the sea of puns, barroom songs, ads, slogans, jingles, sermons, and scholarly lectures, is forcibly reminded that this world exists. The artist/alchemist knows that the highest goal is found in the foulest substance, that it is all about us all the time, that it is buried, like the letter in the *Wake,* in a dung-heap, but will not, upon extracting the letter or the gold, pretend that the dung-heap does not exist.

Finnegans Wake is Joyce's alchemical Philosopher's Stone. It is not a transcendent realm removed from the world, which is what the Symbolists, Yeats, and others sought in alchemy and the occult; nor is it life transmuted into gold, the ordinary perception of the aim of alchemy. Part of Joyce's intention in the *Wake* was to explode our preconceived, categorized ways of looking at things and to reconcile dualities. The *Wake* transforms the elements of life into art, but never renounces its origins; it originates in and returns to the rubbish heap of the world.

Joyce consciously and deliberately chose alchemy as a central metaphor for *Finnegans Wake.* His method of composition in the book could be described as "layering": he began with a basic idea or situation, later adding layers of allusions, word plays, languages. Thomas Connolly states that in *Finnegans Wake*:

> . . . his method resembled that of an expert Japanese lacquerer who begins with a basic coat and then, layer upon layer, builds

> up his medium so that the final product is a highly polished surface that reveals a warm and rich depth down to the basic wood.[14]

In the most important section of the *Wake* in which alchemy and writing are connected (182.30–186.18), Joyce added virtually all the alchemical allusions at one time, proving that he intended them to form a recognizable and meaningful pattern. In British Library MS ADD 47471b, pages 62–64, a second draft in pencil, probably written in 1924, the alchemical layer is absent, although there are several references which later became part of the alchemical context when the body of alchemical allusions was added. Shem's blasphemously Eucharistic formation of his ink is already in evidence, but it had not yet occurred to Joyce to show that Eucharistic transubstantiation and alchemical transmutation reflected the same process.

British Library MS ADD 47474, pages 11–13, a fair copy in ink, sent to Harriet Shaw Weaver and postmarked 8 February 1924, adds nothing of alchemical interest except the word "transaccidentated" and an emphasis on the way in which Shem makes his ink; but in MS ADD 47474, part 2, pages 30–32, nearly all of the alchemical references are evident. This is a first typescript with many additions and corrections, dated February 1924 on the basis of a letter to Harriet Weaver.[15] Many of the additions, in a large hand in pencil, concern alchemy. Shem's address is here first given as "one Brimstone Walk, Asia in Ireland," and a large section which very obviously portrays Shem as an alchemist is added:

> Of course our low hero was a selfvaleter by choice of need so up he got [up] whatever is meant by a kitchenette and fowlhouse for the sake of [eggs which [the jokesmith] brooled and cocked and potched in an athanor with cinnamon and locusts and beeswax and liquorice and Carageen moss and blaster of Barry's and Yellownan's embrocation and stardust and Sinner's tears

> [chanting his cantraps] abracadabra calubra culorum (his oewfs à la Madame Gabrielle de l'Eglise, his oewfs à la Mistress B. de B. Meinfelde, his oewfs à la Sulphate de Soude, his oewfs sowtay sowmonay à la Monseigneur, his soufflosion à la Mère Puard, his Frideggs à la Tricarême)] in what was meant for a closet.[16]

Shem cooks his eggs in an athanor, an alchemical furnace, chanting a magical formula to aid in his work. This draft also calls Shem "the first till last alshemist," adds "sublimation," an important alchemical process and a clue to Joyce's method, and introduces the idea of "circling the square," another alchemical idea.

The fact that Joyce may not have read widely and deeply in alchemical texts and histories does not detract from the significance of these allusions. In exploring the relationship of alchemy to the *Wake,* we should follow Joyce's own partly ironic advice to a friend in reference to Vico's *Scienza Nuova*: "I would not pay overmuch attention to these theories, beyond using them for all they are worth" (*Letters I,* 241). Alchemy serves not only as a metaphor for the artistic process, but also as a source or analogue for many of the major themes of the *Wake,* including incest, colors, forgery, death and rebirth, the dream form, the use of excrement, the Golden Age, number symbolism, the macrocosm-microcosm theory, and the reconciliation of opposites.

I have divided my study thematically, with sections on the use of excrement, the macrocosm-microcosm philosophy, numbers, colors, and ingredients, because I believe that this arrangement reflects Joyce's method of composition and the way in which the alchemical allusions function in the *Wake.* Joyce did not read an alchemical text and then pattern *Finnegans Wake* after it; rather, he began with a series of ideas, themes, and sketches for the *Wake* and used alchemy as one of several metaphors and reference patterns to support these motifs.[17] This thematic method results in the juxtaposition and alchemical identification, explanation, and explication (echoes of the *Wake*'s jury of twelve!) of widely separated references from the *Wake,* which may make the reader wonder whether the references are truly alchemical or how such scattered elements can belong to one pattern. I have tried to overcome this problem by giving a sense of the context of each allusion and the way in which it works in the alchemical theme. Also, not all words, phrases, or motifs which could possibly pertain to alchemy have been considered here; only if other references occur nearby and the allusion adds meaningfully to the texture of the passage is it included. In most cases the allusions do come in clusters, suggesting that they function as part of the alchemical motif.

The alchemical allusions do not fully illuminate the many rooms, passageways, and labyrinths which make up the edifice of *Finnegans Wake*; they do strengthen various motifs, suggest a view of the artist, and throw a small beam of light into a few dark corners. Many of the alchemical references and themes, including resurrection, incest, the four old men, Thoth, and the hen, have several other sources, but no one source excludes or cancels out the others; *Finnegans Wake* does not allow the reader to fall back on comfortable beliefs and presuppositions, including the idea that a book has a correct interpretation.[18] In the *Wake* Joyce moved toward a joyful culinary inclusiveness in which the colors, textures, smells, and flavors of the various ingredients combine with and complement each other. In I.7, a chapter about the artist and artistic creation, we are reminded that:

> . . . the more carrots you chop, the more turnips you slit, the more murphies you peel, the more onions you cry over, the more bullbeef you butch, the more mutton you crackerhack, the more potherbs you pound, the fiercer the fire and the longer your spoon and the harder you gruel with more grease to your elbow the merrier fumes your new Irish stew. (190.03–09)

The Excremental Vision: Spiritual and Physical Alchemy

Finnegans Wake is a rubbish heap. In spite of all the controversy and confusion concerning this book, that fact at least remains muddily clear. It is "the muddest thick that was ever heard dump" (296.20–21). The author "dumptied the wholeborrow of rubbages on to soil here" (17.04–05), creating "a homelike cottage of elvanstone with droppings of biddies, stinkend pusshies, moggies' duggies, rotten witchawubbles, festering rubbages and beggars' bullets, if not worse" (79.29–32). It consists, as does Shem's art, of varied elements, including human excretions of all sorts:

> . . . once current puns, quashed quotatoes, messes of mottage, unquestionable issue papers, seedy ejaculations, limerick damns, crocodile tears, spilt ink, blasphematory spits, stale shestnuts, schoolgirls', young ladies', milkmaids', washerwomen's, shopkeepers' wives, merry widows', ex nuns', vice abbess's, pro virgins', super whores', silent sisters', Charleys' aunts', grandmothers', mothers'-in-laws', fostermothers', godmothers' garters, tress clippings from right, lift and cintrum, worms of snot, toothsome pickings, cans of Swiss condensed bilk, highbrow lotions . . . (183.22–31).

Another fact also remains clear—that "every person, place and thing in the chaosmos of Alle anyway connected with the gobblydumped turkery was moving and changing every part of the time" (118.21–23). Wherever else they might disagree, readers of the book would have to agree that in *Finnegans Wake* nothing, including language, identity, story, or style remains constant; each thing constantly metamorphoses into something else, including, and perhaps especially, its opposite. However, the rubbish heap of *Finnegans Wake* "is not a miseffectual whyacinthinous riot of blots and blurs and bars and balls and hoops and wriggles and juxtaposed jottings linked by spurts of speed: it only looks as like it as damn it" (118.28–31). *Finnegans Wake* also represents the very antithesis of a garbage dump, an ordered work of art.

Since the artist is an alchemist in *Finnegans Wake* and the writing of the book is an alchemical process, the process of alchemical transformation sheds light on that which takes place in *Finnegans Wake.* As already noted, some alchemists used vile substances in the attempt to make gold; similarly, the alchemical goal, the Philosopher's Stone, had a dual aspect. It was the lowest substance and yet the most valuable, the most common and yet the hardest to be found. Janus Lacinius says of the Stone: "They [the Sages] call it the vilest and commonest of all things, which is found among the refuse in the street and on the dunghill; yet they add that it cannot be obtained without considerable expense. They seem to say in the same breath that it is the vilest and that it is the most precious of all substances."[1] The Stone, states Edward Kelly, is "buried not only in the earth, but in a dung heap, and the common streets; for, as the Sages say, it is buried in the streets. This, says the Sage, is the thing which all have, and yet there is no greater secret under heaven, by which diseases are cured, metals transmuted, and all things accomplished."[2]

The dung-heap which is the repository of the letter and the starting and ending point for literature in *Finnegans Wake* derives partially from alchemy.[3] The Mutt-Jute dialogue revolves largely around the controversy of the dump—whether it is merely a dump, or is also a treasure trove, "A middenhide hoard of objects!" (19.08). Someone "dumptied the wholeborrow of rubbages on to soil here" (17.04–05), as noted before, and, as Jute points out, Clontarf field was formed by filling it in with rubbage.[4] A similar collection of refuse has gone into making of this mound:

> Countlessness of livestories have netherfallen by this plage, flick as flowflakes, litters from aloft, like a waast wizzard all of whirlworlds. . . . Hereinunder lyethey. Llarge by the smal an' everynight life olso th'estrange, babylone the greatgrandhotelled with tit tit tittlehouse, alp on earwig, drukn on ild, likeas equal to anequal in this sound seemetery which iz leebez luv. (17.26–36)

Like the alchemical *lapis,* contraries compose this rubbish heap—the great and the small, ALP and HCE, sound and sight. Thus, the dump leads to resurrection—"being humus the same roturns" (18.05).

More significant for its relationship to alchemy is the fact that literature also arises from this dump. The hen digs up the letter from a dung-heap in *Finnegans Wake,* and the alphabet comes from a similar heap. "From the litter comes the letter as from the dump (18.16–35) come letters. Literature, including the *Wake,* is essence of dump; and woman, the Muse's agent, if not the Muse, is collector of rubbish and its renewer."[5] Literature is conceived in the "allaphbed" (18.18) of the dump, which contains "olives, beets, kimmells, dollies, alfrids, beatties, cormacks and daltons" (19.08–09).

The *Wake* manifests the idea that the origins of art lie in the dump of this world in many ways. The Museyroom tour guide continually exhorts his followers to "(Stoop) . . . (please stoop) . . . (please to stoop) . . . (O stoop to please!)" (18.17–19.10) if they wish to read the "world" written here.

Martha Clifford's confusion of "word" and "world" (*U* 77) comes into play here, for literature is the "other world." But, we must stoop to understand it, not gaze upward to the celestial. Literature has firm roots in this world. "Indeed, if you are 'abcedminded' and can stoop enough, you can interpret *Finnegans Wake,* which, like the earth itself, is a lettered dump and a letter to someone composed of dumped letters," states Tindall.[6]

The insistence of *Finnegans Wake* on its origins in terms of alchemy and the dung-heap indicates that alchemy acts as a primary metaphor for the artistic process in this book. Joyce's view is that of the alchemists, who, although they search for their goal in rubbish, do not aim at total transcendence. Jung quotes and interprets Morienus' emphasis on the acceptance of the low origins of the Hermetic Art: "'Take that which is trodden underfoot upon the dung-heap; if you do not, when you wish to climb the stairs, you will fall down upon your head.' By which he means that if a man will not accept what he has cast aside, it will force itself upon him the moment he wishes to climb higher."[7] To reinforce the parallel between alchemy and writing, the elements of literature are cooked alchemically after the Mutt-Jute "middenhide hoard" discussion to produce Gutenberg and the printed word (20.05–11).

An alchemical connection between a dunghill and rebirth may have also influenced Joyce. Some workmen unknowingly threw some alchemical Red Tincture onto a dung-heap, which, when spread on a field, resulted in an extraordinarily fertile crop (see p. 38). In a like manner, in *Finnegans Wake* the filling in of Clontarf field with rubbish leads to the birth of the alphabet and subsequently of literature. The hen gathers the pieces of the letter from a littered battlefield (11.08–28); literature, including *Finnegans Wake,* arises from a dump (16.33–20.18); the letter, "the first babe of reconcilement," is buried again by Kate (79.27–80.19); and the letter is dug up from a midden once again by Belinda of the Dorans (110.22–112.02). Litter, the letter, letters, and literature move through continuous cycles of transformation. When the hen rescues the letter on pages 110–12, the resurrection of the manuscript leads to a general alchemical resurrection, the "Golden Age" of Paracelsus, including both material and spiritual rebirth (see p. 50).

The garbage heap of *Finnegans Wake,* then, is transformed into art, just as the alchemists transformed the vilest substance into the highest goal, the Philosopher's Stone. Or, to be more exact, *Finnegans Wake* is *both* rubbish and gold. This relates to another alchemical duality, one which has importance in Joyce's view of the artist in *Finnegans Wake.* As previously mentioned, alchemy had both a physical and a spiritual or mystical side. The 11th edition of the *Encyclopedia Britannica* suggests that the alchemy which grew out of Alexandrian Egypt began with practical methods for making alloys and coloring metals. Mystical interpretations of the processes, the identification of the metals with the planets, the use of magic formulas, the concept of each person as a microcosm reflecting the macrocosm, and even the concept of transmutation resulted from contact with Greek philosophy and Eastern influences. Later, some authors claimed that the perfection of the human soul was just as or more important than the perfection of base metals into gold. These two aspects intermingled, but they tended to become polarized; therefore, exoteric and esoteric alchemy, at least in theory, became somewhat distinct. The late nineteenth- and early twentieth-century revivalists of alchemy, whom Joyce probably read, emphasized the difference, indicating their preference for the spiritual and demeaning the physical side:

> Simply stated, Hermeticism, or its synonym Alchemy, was in its primary intention and office the philosophic and exact science of the regeneration of the human soul from its present sense-

immersed state into the perfection and nobility of that divine condition in which it was originally created. Secondarily and incidentally, as will presently appear, it carried with it a knowledge of the way in which the life-essence of things belonging to the sub-human kingdoms—the metallic *genera* in particular—can, correspondingly, be intensified and raised to a nobler form than that in which it exists in its present natural state. It is to this secondary aspect only that the popular mind turns when Alchemy is mentioned, unaware of the subject's larger and primary intention.[8]

Yeats expresses a similar view in "Rosa Alchemica":

I had discovered, early in my researches, that their [the alchemists'] doctrine was no merely chemical phantasy, but a philosophy they applied to the world, to the elements and to man himself; and that they sought to fashion gold out of common metals merely as part of an universal transmutation of all things into some divine and imperishable substance.[9]

The split, however, occurred centuries earlier and can be seen in the alchemical texts themselves. The seventeenth-century collection *The Hermetic Museum* widened the gap; most of the texts included in this book rail against those who use hair, urine, eggs, and other vile substances in their pursuit of the Stone. In fact, some treatises go so far as to deplore not only the use of these common substances, but also of all physical or chemical ingredients and equipment. Instead, they espouse a vague mystical process having nothing to do with the laboratory:

With all these useless and unnecessary experiments the true Alchemists will have nothing to do. They follow the method pursued by Nature in the veins of the earth, which is very simple, and includes no solutions, putrefactions, coagulations, or anything of the kind. Can Nature, in the heart of the earth, where the metals do grow and receive increase, have anything

> corresponding to all those pseudo-alchemistical instruments, alembics, retorts, circulatory and sublimatory phials, fires, and other materials, such as cobbler's wax, salt, arsenic, mercury, sulphur, and so forth? Can all these things really be necessary for the growth and increase of the metals? It is surprising that any one not entirely bereft of his senses can spend many years in the study of alchemy, and yet never get beyond those foolish and frivolous solutions, coagulations, putrefactions, distillations, while Nature is so simple and unsophisticated in her methods.[10]

Some later texts derided the alchemists who took the idea of the base origin of the Stone too literally as shortsighted fools. Those who sought the *lapis* in "female menstruums, the seminal fluid, eggs, hairs, urine and similar things"[11] were spurned and given the mocking title "puffers" for their belief that if a transmutation had not been effected, it was merely because their fires had not been hot enough.

Parallel to the alchemical "puffers" in Joyce's theory of art are those who look on the world with no wonder, who see in it no mystery. They merely accumulate facts, and like the mixtures of urine, feces, hair, and eggs of the literal-minded alchemists, the result of their collections remains an accumulation of disparate elements. Joyce parodies such minds in *Finnegans Wake*. For instance, the textual exegesis of the letter on pages 113.34–125.23 examines a multitude of facts, including the direction of the lines, the type of paper used, the fact that it is not signed, the calligraphy, the dialectical variations, and the punctuation, yet sheds no real light on the meaning or significance of the letter. Sir Edward Sullivan's introduction to the Book of Kells is also parodied, as are Marxian, Freudian, and Jungian critics. The letter is *Finnegans Wake*—the reference to Joyce's symbols for HCE and ALP (119.17, 19) makes this clear; therefore, this passage clues the reader as to what *Finnegans Wake* is *not*, and warns against a short-sighted, literal-minded way of reading it.

Some alchemists warn others away from the literal path once they have seen the light themselves.

> I can speak from bitter experience. For I, too, toiled for many years in accordance with those sophistic methods, and endeavoured to reach the coveted goal by sublimation, distillation, calcination, circulation, and so forth, and to fashion the Stone out of substances such as urine, salt, altrament, alum, etc. I have tried hard to evolve it out of hairs, eggs, bones, and all manner of herbs; out of arsenic, mercury, and sulphur, and all the minerals and metals. I have striven to elicit it by means of aqua fortis and alkali. I have spent nights and days in dissolving, coagulating, amalgamating, and precipitating. Yet from all those things I derived neither profit nor joy. I had hoped much from the quintessence, but it disappointed me like the rest.[12]

The tendency to eschew all laboratory processes exhibited by this discouraged alchemist became more pronounced, until the Hermetic Art became completely spiritualized, refined out of the laboratory and almost out of existence. Whereas the aim of some of the alchemists and their supporters was clearly monetary, those who believed that the end of alchemy was spiritual condemned the idea of material gain so much as to deny it had ever been part of alchemy. Alchemical processes and their goal became internalized, and the efforts of previous alchemists over their retorts were seen as wholly metaphorical. Although there is no agreement as to which came first, the spiritual metaphor or the literal egg-shaped Hermetic *vas,* what is important is the division of what had once been a unified tradition.

C. G. Jung's work on the unconscious led him to an investigation of alchemy and alchemical symbolism. Finding remarkable similarities between the symbolism of the Hermetic Art and the dreams of modern patients, he also asserts that alchemy was a mystic philosophy as well as a precursor of chemistry, a view which, as we have seen, has much support in the alchemical texts themselves. What Jung views as the central image of alchemy, the *coniunctio,* the mating or Royal Marriage, operates on both these levels:

> The alchemical image of the *coniunctio,* whose practical importance was proved at a later stage of development, is equally valuable from the psychological point of view: that is to say, it plays the same role in the exploration of the darkness of the psyche as it played in the investigation of the riddle of matter.[13]

For Jung, alchemy represents the individuation process that he describes in *The Psychology of the Transference*; it is the creation of a self. Jung states: "I may define 'self' as the totality of the conscious and unconscious psyche, but this totality transcends our vision; it is a veritable *lapis invisibilitatis.*"[14] According to Jung, the alchemist projected his unconscious into matter; thus, the material process which occurred in the alchemical *vas* paralleled his own psychic process. Jung explains:

> I mean by this that while working on his chemical experiments the operator had certain psychic experiences which appeared to him as the particular behaviour of the chemical process. Since it was a question of projection, he was naturally unconscious of the fact that the experience had nothing to do with matter itself (that is, with matter as we know it today). He experienced his projection as a property of matter; but what he was in reality experiencing was his own unconscious.[15]

This suggests the alchemical belief in correspondences among different levels of the universe ("as above, so below"), but makes these correspondences a result of the alchemists' own psychic needs and projections rather than a metaphysical statement about the way things are.

In Jungian theory the self is the container of all opposites, "a union of opposites *par excellence,*" the archetype of the God-image within us. Indefinite, indeterminate, and variegated, this imprint on the unconscious cannot be filled by a single religious figure:

> It is altogether inconceivable that there could be any definite figure capable of expressing archetypal indefiniteness. For this reason I have found myself obliged to give the corresponding archetype the psychological name of the "self"—a term on the one hand definite enough to convey the essence of human wholeness and on the other hand indefinite enough to express the indescribable and indeterminable nature of this wholeness. The paradoxical qualities of the term are a reflection of the fact that wholeness consists partly of the conscious man and partly of the unconscious man. But we cannot define the latter or indicate his boundaries. Hence in its scientific usage the term "self" refers neither to Christ nor to the Buddha but to the totality of the figures that are its equivalent, and each of these figures is a symbol of the self.[16]

This accounts for the behavior of characters in *Finnegans Wake*; they merge into each other, change identities, and take on the characteristics of others. Each main character is a type of Jungian "self," both individual and general. ALP is Anna Livia Plurabelle, wife of Humphrey Chimpden Earwicker, yet she is also Eve, the Liffey, all rivers, the hen. Joyce takes a cue for his literary technique from this concept of archetypal indefiniteness. Each of his characters represents a Jungian "self," the union of conscious and unconscious sought by the alchemists in their work.

Although unaware of the projection of their psychic predispositions into the matter with which they were working, the alchemists were still able to create the "self" by uniting the conscious and the unconscious. According to Jung, this was because they realized, even if obscurely, "that the essential secret of the art lies hidden in the human mind."

Alchemical writers continually insist on the importance of the mental and moral state of the worker to the success of the work—the alchemist must be pure in heart and mind, devout, cheerful, humane, and charitable.[17]

Jung quotes several works which "prove that during the practical work certain events of an hallucinatory or visionary nature were perceived, which cannot be anything but projections of unconscious contents."[18] The alchemists *saw* the contents of the unconscious, then; they were not completely cut off from it. Because of these visual manifestations the dream form became important to the literature of alchemy; in some texts the dream acts merely as a literary convention, but in others the dream vision functions as an essential part of the alchemical process.

The result of modern science has been to "despiritualize nature through its so-called objective knowledge of matter,"[19] making such visions and such direct contact with the unconscious impossible. Therefore, the union of conscious and unconscious must now be accomplished by another means. For Jung dreams are manifestations of unconscious psychic content; hence Jungian psychoanalysis involves making a person aware of the unconscious through dream analysis. The process continues until the dreams indicate that the patient has accepted this side of her/himself, and a new "self" has been born. In *Psychology and Alchemy* Jung interprets such a series of dreams to show that their content is universal, that their progression and use of symbols is alchemical, and that the process undergone is that of individuation.

Finnegans Wake also takes the form of a dream: "As Joyce informed a friend later, he conceived of his book as the dream of old Finn, lying in death beside the river Liffey and watching the history of Ireland and the world—past and future—flow through his mind like flotsam on the river of life."[20] *Finnegans Wake* deals with naturalistic events, such as an evening in a Chapelizod pub, but also with unconscious, repressed material, such as HCE's incestuous desires toward Issy. The book, then, attempts to reveal the wholeness of experience, the union of conscious and unconscious, the simultaneous operation of physical and spiritual events aimed at in the alchemical process. Joyce's alchemical artist, however, is still a sham. The dream allows Joyce to deal with things in a way that our rational categorizing minds do not, but it is no more a revelation of an objective truth than were the visions or transmutations of the alchemists. As Margot Norris points out, Joyce's portrait of the artist changed as a result of the shift of his interest from the conscious to the unconscious: ". . . he was increasingly forced to recognize the inauthenticity and self-delusion that the artist shares with the philistine. In the world of the dream, every individual is a demon and an angel, a pharisee and a holy man, a charlatan and an artist."[21] The way in which the alchemical metaphor illuminates this view of thc artist will be developed in more detail in the remainder of this study.

But besides being a dream, *Finnegans Wake* is also, according to Ruth Von Phul, a "confessional" book in which Joyce confesses and reveals all about himself in order to come to terms with himself. In fact, this critic reads all of Joyce's works this way, *Finnegans Wake* being the extreme example of his urge to confess and yet to conceal.[22] Following this theory, *Finnegans Wake* becomes, in a sense, Joyce's analyst. Joyce refused to consult Jung at the request of one of his benefactors, Mrs. McCormick, who then cut off his monthly stipend.[23] When a hostile psychoanalytic inquisitor accuses a character in the *Wake* of having "homosexual catheis of empathy between narcissism of the expert and steatopygic invertedness" and orders, "Get yourself psychoanolised!", he replies:

—O, begor, I want no expert nursis symaphy from yours broons quadroons and I can psoakoonaloose myself any time I want (the fog follow you all!) without your interferences or any other pigeonstealer. (522.33–36)

Perhaps Joyce was attempting to come to terms with his unconscious in his writings; if so, the transference which occurs between doctor and patient would then occur between Joyce and his book. In *The Psychology of the Transference* Jung develops the theory that the process of transference is that of the union of opposites or the Royal Marriage which occurs in alchemy. Therefore, if *Finnegans Wake* is a confessional work, Joyce underwent, through the process of transference or individuation, the process undergone by the alchemist.

The theory that Joyce works out his internal conflicts in his books does have textual support. He himself calls *Finnegans Wake* "that letter selfpenned to one's other" (489.33–34), "this nonday diary, this allnights newseryreel" (489.35). Also, Clive Hart states that Joyce's use of autobiography in his works is "the most powerful symbolic exorcism," and attributes Joyce's technique to this need to work out his conflicts:

> As soon as the personal experience had been externalized by committal to paper and by the open confession in the market-place which publication represented, the drives and conflicts temporarily evaporated and interest dissolved. Joyce, a little masochistic, inclined to sexual perversion, and in exile from a homeland he both loved and despised, could, of course, never rid himself for long of his deep-seated emotional conflicts, but whenever the need for artistic purgation arose again, fresh techniques were necessary; the same magic could not be made to work twice. On each occasion a more potent exorcism was called for, involving greater complexity, more difficult labyrinths from which to escape, and, above all, the objectification and rationalisation of more and more personal involvement.[24]

Perhaps that is why for his last work Joyce called on alchemy to help him, a process that in the past had united the opposites and reconciled the forces within a person to form the "self." Such a view, however, must be careful to distinguish Joyce from his creation. He may have used his works for personal exorcism, but Joyce never loses artistic control, nor can he be identified with any of the characters he creates. If Joyce acted as his own psychoanalyst, he did so with a degree of humor and distance. He used any theory or technique which was useful to him, used it for all it was worth and for his own purposes.

Joyce's use of alchemy exemplifies his desire to account for all aspects of existence in another way as well. In Jung's view alchemy is compensatory to Christianity. He states:

> The point is that alchemy is rather like an undercurrent to the Christianity that ruled on the surface. It is to this surface as the dream is to consciousness, and just as the dream compensates the conflicts of the conscious mind, so alchemy endeavours to fill in the gaps left open by the Christian tension of opposites.[25]

The Christian deity, the Trinity, is masculine, since uneven numbers are traditionally regarded as masculine. Thus, in the alchemical axiom of Maria, "One becomes two, two becomes three, and out of the third comes the one as the fourth," "the even numbers which signify the feminine principle, earth, the regions under the earth, and evil itself are interpolated between the uneven numbers of the Christian dogma."[26] A chthonic deity counters the spiritual Christian one. The Church, however, regarded alchemy not as a necessary complement, but as heretical. The *Wake*'s version of the conflict includes an allusion to Zosimus, the third-century Alexandrian alchemist and the first alchemical writer whose personal identity is known: the "sissymusses and the zozzymusses" (154.08) shrink with fear at the bellowing of the Mookse, the Pope, and the Church in their militant aspects trying to take over Ireland.

Yet, Joyce uses alchemy overall in *Finnegans Wake* to round out the one-sided Christian dogma and the conscious, rational side of our lives, to compensate for the aspects of life they ignore. As alchemy is the "dream" of Christianity, so *Finnegans Wake* is the "dream" of our categorized, compartmentalized everyday lives. Whereas in "real life" people are individual, have stable identities, and live in a certain time period, in *Finnegans Wake* characters are also archetypal, have shifting identities, and are not tied to a specified time period.

Since alchemy is compensatory to Christianity, alchemists often compare the Stone to Christ or portray the alchemical work as the Mass. Jung says of a fifteenth-century work by Nicholas Melchior: "We can clearly discern from the text . . . that he felt the alchemistic process to be the equivalent of the process of transubstantiation in the Mass, and that for that very reason he felt the need of representing his experience in the form of the Mass."[27] Therefore, when Shem the "alshemist" transaccidentates himself in the process of his art, he combines both Christian Eucharistic transubstantiation and alchemical transmutation.

The alchemical metaphor further illuminates Joyce's view of the artist. By his emphasis on the union of opposites, by his insistence that *Finnegans Wake* is a rubbish heap yet a work of art, Joyce returns to the unified alchemical tradition and to a view of the universe in which the stars, human beings, animals, metals, and stones are related to and influence each other. Joyce did not "believe" in alchemy, but he believed in the necessity for integrating the physical and the spiritual. Joyce's art is both literal and symbolic, concerned with the details of everyday life, yet mythical and archetypal. Humphrey Chimpden Earwicker is a Chapelizod pubkeeper, yet he is *also* "Here Comes Everybody," Adam, Napoleon, Humpty Dumpty, and all heroes of all time; in *Finnegans Wake* both levels are constantly and simultaneously real. One of the reasons for the constant shifting of identities is that for Joyce neither an art which absolutely eschews the everyday world nor one which is completely mired in it is true art. For Stephen Dedalus of *Portrait* the artist forges "out of the sluggish matter of the earth a new soaring impalpable imperishable being" (*P* 169), yet in Stephen's villanelle the circumstances which inspired the poem are completely absent—there are no library steps, no Gaelic lessons, no priest, no real woman. Desire prompts the poem, yet that physical feeling has disappeared, transmuted into an "eucharistic hymn" in which Stephen as priest transforms his experience into an eternal abstract form. The moment has something magnificent about it, as does Stephen's vision of the girl on the beach, yet Joyce's technique implies a criticism of this type of artist and of the entire "art for art's sake" movement. Stephen wants to escape completely from this world, but escape is impossible, as the reference to Icarus points out. When Stephen realizes his calling to the priesthood of art:

> His heart trembled; his breath came faster and a wild spirit passed over his limbs as though he were soaring sunward. His heart trembled in an ecstasy of fear and his soul was in flight. His soul was soaring in an air beyond the world and the body he knew was purified in a breath and delivered of incertitude and made radiant and commingled with the element of the spirit. An ecstasy of flight made radiant his eyes and wild his breath and tremulous and wild and radiant his windwept limbs.

Immediately, however, the banter of the boys,

> —One! Two! . . . Look out!
> —O, cripes, I'm drownded! (*P* 169)

shows the futility of the attempt to escape. At the end of the novel, by calling on Dedalus as his father, Stephen again identifies himself with the fallen Icarus.

The attempt to transcend this world completely by means of art is bound to fail. The antidote to this attitude is Leopold Bloom. Bloom's attitude to art is that of the literal-minded alchemists; he, like they, uses the most mundane substances for his art and hopes to receive financial reward for his efforts. He wants to write a completely realistic piece, one based on Molly's comments while dressing. After reading *Matcham's Masterstroke* and defecating in a most satisfactory manner, Bloom's thoughts turn to his own literary ambitions, and he thinks:

> Time I used to try jotting down on my cuff what she said dressing. . . . Timing her. 9.15. Did Roberts pay you yet? 9.20. What had Gretta Conroy on? 9.23. What possessed me to buy this comb? 9.24. I'm swelled after that cabbage. (*U* 69)

Bloom realizes, though, that "It wouldn't pan out somehow." (*U* 69)

Bloom's art is the very antithesis of Stephen's, or at least of Stephen's aesthetic theory; it is utilitarian; it aims toward an end. He turns literature into one of the useful arts. In the passage cited above his aim is monetary—he envies Mr. Beaufoy the money he has been paid for his story. In "Ithaca" we get a fuller catalogue of Bloom's literary efforts, both critical and creative. While sipping cocoa "he reflected on the pleasures derived from literature of instruction rather than of amusement as he himself had applied to the works of William Shakespeare more than once for the solution of difficult problems in imaginary or real life" (*U* 677). Bloom's "first piece of original verse written by him, potential poet, at the age of 11" (*U* 677) is also goal-oriented, since he writes it in the hope of winning the prize money offered by a newspaper.

But Bloom's most ambitious literary efforts are directed toward an end other than the financial. While courting Molly he had written a poem for her:

> What acrostic upon the abbreviation of his first name had he (kinetic poet) sent to Miss Marion Tweedy on the 14 February 1888?
>
> Poets oft have sung in rhyme
> Of music sweet their praise divine.
> Let them hymn it nine times nine.
> Dearer far than song or wine,
> You are mine. The world is mine.
>
> (*U* 678)

Bloom is pointedly called a "kinetic poet"—the type of artist Stephen deplores in *Portrait,* and related to those alchemists whose aim was material.

While Bloom has the qualities of humanity and charity which Stephen lacks, and while there is "a touch of the artist about old Bloom" (*U* 235), he will never be a real artist. In fact, although in Joyce's work there are many artist figures, there are none capable of uniting the material and the spiritual, rubbish and art; that is to say, none are capable of writing the works of Joyce. Shem seems to accomplish a true artistic creation; he takes the particular and makes it universal, and he overcomes time and space, writing with "gallic acid on iron ore" on his own body, "till by its corrosive sublimation one continuous present tense integument slowly unfolded all marryvoising moodmoulded cyclewheeling history (thereby, he said, reflecting from his own individual person life unlivable, transaccidentated through the slow fires of consciousness into a dividual chaos, perilous, potent, common to allflesh, human only, mortal)" (185.36–186.06). However, "with each word that would not pass away the squidself which he had squirtscreened from the crystalline world waned chagreenold and doriangrayer in its dudhud"

(186.06–08). The reference to Dorian Gray puts Shem's art in proper perspective. Art cannot substitute for life. Marguerite Harkness' comments on Stephen apply equally to Shem and to all such artists:

> Stephen, like Dorian, tries to make his life into art, forgetting the legitimate and inescapable demands of his emotions. His mother warns him and the reader of the limitations he has imposed upon himself and his adaptation to life when she prays that he may come to understand "what the heart is and what it feels" . . . Through the use of this implied analogy [to Dorian Gray] Joyce indicates one of Stephen's future difficulties and the incompleteness of his assumed life pattern.[28]

The elements of *Finnegans Wake* are the most commonplace of things—ads, nursery rhymes, lectures, guided tours, homework, children's games, songs. They are constantly changing, being transformed, transmuted, metamorphosed into more than that; still, however, they also remain what they are. Part of the joy of reading *Finnegans Wake* is the recognition of these elements—we smile, congratulate ourselves, annotate our margins—yet *Finnegans Wake* also transmutes them into a type of literary gold. For me both levels are simultaneously and equally real. Joyce resembles those alchemists who worked on both the physical and spiritual levels; that is why he is both the most realistic and the most symbolic of writers.

"As Above, So Below," and Death and Rebirth

The two aspects of alchemy, the spiritual and the physical, spring from the world view of the Hermetic Art; a belief in the unity of the cosmos, that macrocosm and microcosm reflect each other, was the core of alchemical philosophy. This doctrine appears in the *Tabula Smaragdina,* the *Emerald Tablet,* of Hermes, regarded as the father of alchemy. The Greeks identified Hermes with Thoth, "the Egyptian god of letters, invention and wisdom . . . the mouthpiece and recorder of the gods, and arbiter of their disputes."[1] Secretary to Osiris, Thoth reputedly invented speech and writing. "Since magic depends upon words, he became magus-in-chief and, under Greek auspices, the Logos or creator of things."[2] Most alchemists refer to the father of their art as Hermes Trismegistus ("Thrice-Greatest"); "after him later alchemists called their work the 'hermetic art,' and the seal of Hermes, which they placed upon their vessels, is the origin of the common phrase 'hermetically sealed.'"[3]

The *Emerald Tablet* had a sufficiently mystical origin:

> In a work attributed to Albertus Magnus, but which is probably spurious, we are told that Alexander the Great found the tomb of Hermes in a cave near Hebron. This tomb contained an

emerald table—'The Smaragdine Table'—on which were inscribed the following thirteen sentences in Phoenician characters:—

1. I speak not fictitious things, but what is true and most certain.
2. What is below is like that which is above, and what is above is like that which is below, to accomplish the miracles of one thing.
3. And as all things were produced by the mediation of one Being, so all things were produced from this one thing by adaptation.
4. Its father is the Sun, its mother the Moon; the wind carries it in its belly, its nurse is the earth.
5. It is the cause of all perfection throughout the whole world.
6. Its power is perfect if it be changed into earth.
7. Separate the earth from the fire, the subtle from the gross, acting prudently and with judgment.
8. Ascend with the greatest sagacity from the earth to heaven, and then again descend to the earth, and unite together the power of things superior and things inferior. Thus you will obtain the glory of the whole world, and all obscurity will fly far away from you.
9. This thing is the fortitude of all fortitude, because it overcomes all subtle things, and penetrates every solid thing.
10. Thus were all things created.
11. Thence proceed wonderful adaptations which are produced in this way.
12. Therefore am I called Hermes Trismegistus, possessing the three parts of the philosophy of the whole world.
13. That which I had to say concerning the operation of the Sun is completed.[4]

Shortened to "as above, so below," this doctrine permeated alchemy and became the justification for the belief that the macrocosm and microcosm mirrored each other. In Wakean cosmology, it becomes: "The tasks above are as the flasks below, saith the emerald canticle of Hermes" (263.21–22). Like Hermes' macrocosm/microcosm theory, this passage concerns the difficult philosophical problem of things being different and yet the same. Or, as the Gripes, considering the Hermetic *vas* as the Philosophic Egg (see p. 51), puts it: "And my spetial inexshellsis the belowing things ab ove" (154.35). In alchemy this doctrine had several manifestations, such as the belief that the planets influenced earthly things, and that parallel processes operated in metals, in people, and in the heavens.

The many references to Hermes and Thoth in *Finnegans Wake* and the association of these two gods with writing indicate Joyce's association of writing and alchemy.[5] Boldereff identifies Thoth as the teacher who first taught the artist to "pose the pen" (303.02). Generally, Shem acts as Hermes/Thoth, but the association does not remain constant: "As inventor of letters, Thoth is a role natural to Shem the Penman . . . but in *FW* III, i, ii, things move backward, roles are exchanged. Thoth is identical with Hermes-Mercury, god of thieves, and is played by Shaun the Post . . . who steals his brother's invention and hawks it as his own. . . ."[6] In his farewell speech to his sister, Shaun pictures himself as "thauthor," "besated upon my tripos . . . picking up airs from th'other over th'ether . . . this night sublime" (452.09–14). Hermes Trismegistus also delivered his oracles from a tripos (*OED*); some alchemists considered the Philosopher's Stone as an ether or quintessence; the "night sublime" might refer to the alchemical process of sublimation. Although Shaun uses high-flown rhetoric throughout and aggrandizes himself and his journey ("it is historically the most glorious mission, secret or profund, through all the annals of our . . . efferfreshpainted livy" 452.17–19), his thoughts and motives are, as always, tied to earth. His paean to heaven soon gives way to a Falstaffian hymn to food, while the remainder of his speech and his sister's reply make it clear that Shaun has been more than a brother to her. After all, he might say, he is merely following the Hermetic dictum, "as above, so below" . . . .

Shaun utilizes alchemy to his advantage in a similar way a

bit later. Having finished his sermon, he seems to collapse. The "twentyaid add one" (469.30) girls unsuccessfully attempt to assist him, but Shaun gives himself "some sort of a hermetic prod or kick to sit up and take notice, which acted like magic" (470.02–03). The magic involves not just Shaun's alchemical rise after his fall, but his sexual one too. Cunningly, "in selfrighting the balance of his corporeity to reexchange widerembrace with the pillarbosom of the Dizzier he loved prettier," he gets nearer his goal, but, "at the summit of his climax," his hat blows off "in a loveblast" and Shaun goes "bucketing after" (471.05–14).

Joyce also transforms the macrocosm-microcosm theory attributed to Hermes and of such importance in alchemy into a literary technique. The fall of Satan, the fall of Adam, the fall of Humpty Dumpty, the fall of Tim Finnegan, and the fall of Humphrey Chimpden Earwicker are one and the same. The method by which Joyce achieves this identification can be demonstrated by "The Ballad of Persse O'Reilly" (44–47). The song is both specific and universal. "*Perce-oreille* is French for 'earwig.'"[7] The title of the ballad thus indicates that it is about HCE as well, as do his initials, found in the phrase "He'll Cheat E'erawan" (46.01), and the fact that the subject of the song has a hump (45.06). Humpty Dumpty and Cromwell are added to this amalgamated man in stanza 1. "Hosty" brings to mind HCE's occupation of tavernkeeper, but also widens his identity to include the religious sacrifice, the Eucharistic host. The Christian symbol of sacrifice is then universalized:

> ". . . the rann, the rann, the king of all ranns . . ."—this echoes a catch sung on December 26, when Irish boys parade around with a dead bird on a pole:
>
> The wren, the wren,
> The king of all birds,
> Saint Stephen's his day,
> Was caught in the furze.

In this ritual, the wren is treated "like a slain god, carried about so all may share its virtue."[8]

On a larger scale, Joyce makes the members of the Earwicker family both microcosmic and macrocosmic. HCE is Humphrey Chimpden Earwicker, owner of a specific pub in a specific time and place, with a family consisting of twin sons, a daughter, and a wife. But he is also "Here Comes Everybody," symbolic of all people at all times and places. The microcosm reflects the macrocosm in *Finnegans Wake*. Archetypal patterns of the fall, incest, sibling rivalry, conquest of the father by the sons, death and rebirth, and others are re-enacted by specific characters in *Finnegans Wake,* but by his constant allusions to other manifestations of these themes in legend, history, story, and song, Joyce keeps both halves of the mirror constantly before us. Just as the union of sulphur and mercury in the alchemical process mirrored on a human level the union of male and female, on a symbolic level the union of King and Queen, and on a cosmic level the union of Sun and Moon, so do the situations and characters in *Finnegans Wake* operate on all levels simultaneously.

Besides being the basis for the microcosm-macrocosm theory, alchemy serves as one of Joyce's sources for many archetypal themes. Although it is impossible to talk of an ur-myth, Joyce attempts in *Finnegans Wake* to get behind individual myths and societal world views to a more all-encompassing and primordial philosophy; that is why no one myth will serve his needs. Although alchemical philosophy derives from many sources, alchemy serves as such an ur-myth in the *Wake* because it deals with such basic concepts as death and rebirth, soul and body, change and unity.

Life-death-rebirth constitutes one of the most basic of all cycles; Joyce made it the primary theme of *Finnegans Wake* because of its universality. Since his aim was to go beyond specific cultural and religious myths, to portray the most elemental features of life, the death-rebirth theme plays the most significant role in the *Wake,* and alchemy serves as one source for this theme.

As with other aspects of alchemy, the processes to be followed for the successful achievement of the goal were ill-defined and the details, names, and order of the processes varied from one alchemist to another. However, a general classification of steps can be outlined. John Read extrapolates the sequence of processes as follows:

(1) Purification of the primitive materials.
(2) Preparation of the proximate materials.
(3) Treatment in the Philosopher's Egg, or Hermetic Vase, with attendant colour changes.
(4) Increasing the potency of the resulting Stone (*multiplication*).
(5) Transmutation (in the operation of *projection*).[9]

Generally the alchemists regarded the first two steps as preliminary and considered the work which took place in the Hermetic Vase as the essential alchemical work. Even so, the texts show variation in the processes to be followed for the achievement of the alchemical goal. In *The Compound of Alchymie* Sir George Ripley gives twelve processes—calcination, solution, separation, conjunction, putrefaction, congelation, cibation, sublimation, fermentation, exaltation, multiplication, and projection, while in *The Fount of Chemical Truth* Philalethes lists the processes of calcination, dissolution, separation, conjunction, putrefaction, distillation, coagulation, sublimation, fixation, and exaltation.[10] Complicating matters further is the fact that: "The adepts were not consistent in their use of terms; their language was apt to be vague; often, also, they attached a mystical significance to the materials, colours, processes, and apparatus of the Great Work."[11] Still, a general movement can be discerned, one which follows the death-rebirth cycle. The substances are blackened or "putrefied," and then, freed from their gross elements, emerge pure and reborn.

In the Aristotelian theory of change everything strives to reach its desired end—the acorn to become an oak tree that will produce more acorns, for example. Inherent in this theory is the idea that each thing contains its end within it; the acorn contains the oak tree. Consonant with this theory, the alchemists believed that all metals were striving to reach their end, which was gold.

> The only thing that distinguishes one metal from another, is its degree of maturity, which is, of course, greatest in the most precious metals; the difference between gold and lead is not one of substance, but of digestion; in the baser metal the coction has not been such as to purge out its metallic impurities. If by any means this superfluous impure matter could be organically removed from the baser metals, they would become gold and silver.[12]

According to a treatise by Edward Kelly, *The Stone of the Philosophers,* metals are classified as "mature" and "immature," the degree of maturity being dependent on the degree of the metal's affinity with fire, the highest element; immature metals are dominated by water. Only the most mature metal has "exactly attained all the activities and properties of fire. Such is gold."[13] The other metals have a tendency toward this perfection and continually strive to reach this state.

The distinction between the body and soul became operative in the attempt to mature metals into gold; the alchemists believed that the soul of gold was caught in the body of earthly metals and could be released in the alchemical process. As one alchemist states:

> Blessed, yea, thrice blessed, is the man to whom Jehovah has revealed the method of preparing that Divine Salt by which the

> metallic or mineral body is corrupted, destroyed, and mortified, while its soul in the meantime is revived for the glorious resurrection of the philosophical body.[14]

Many texts depict the alchemical process as a king rising from a tomb. In a series of pictures in *The New Pearl of Great Price* the son and five servants of a king kneel before him to request their share of power. When the king denies their petition, the son stabs and kills his father, falling into the grave with him. Putrefaction of their bodies takes place, and their bones are cast on the purified earth. "Then the King rises from the tomb, full of the grace of God. His body is now all spiritual and heavenly, and he has power to make all his servants kings."[15]

There is no need to rehearse the importance of death and rebirth in *Finnegans Wake*; however, some specific instances help illuminate the alchemical metaphor. In I.4, which gives a multitude of instances and forms of the death and resurrection of HCE, his grave is described: "This wastohavebeen underground heaven, or mole's paradise which was probably also an inversion of a phallopharos, intended to foster wheat crops" (76.33–35). "Foster" may be a shoemaker of Bath who attested to the efficacy of the alchemical elixir as a fertilizer. When the abbey at Bath was dissolved, William Holway, the prior, hid a vial of the Red Elixir in a wall, but then could not find it again. However, when workmen tore down some stone-work,

> there was a Glasse found in a Wall full of Red Tincture, which being flung away to a dunghill, forthwith coloured it, exceeding red. This dunghill (or Rubish) was afterwards fetched away by Boate by Bathwicke men, and layd in Bathwicke field, and in the places where it was spread, for a long tyme after, the Corne grew wonderfully ranke, thick, and high: insomuch as it was there look'd upon as a wonder. This Belcher and Foster (2 Shoomakers of Bath, who dyed about 20 yeares since) can very well remember. . . .[16]

The association with the dung-heap makes this tale particularly appropriate to *Finnegans Wake.* The Red Tincture which finds its way from the rubbish heap to Bathwicke field becomes an instrument of regeneration, as does the whiskey which wakes Finnegan, and the body of Frazer's priest-king, sacrificed so that the crops of his people will flourish.

Besides the obvious sexual meaning, the above passage also echoes Christ's parable, which Ripley uses to describe the alchemical process of putrefaction in *The Compound of Alchymie*:

> Now begynneth the Chapter of Putrefaccion,
> Wythout whych Pole no sede may multyply,
> Whych must be done only by contynuall accyon
> Of hete in the body, moyst, not manually,
> For Bodies ells may not be alterat naturally:
> Syth Chryst do it wytnes, wythowt the
> grayne of Whete
> Dye in the ground, encrese may thou not gete.[17]

An illustration from the *Viridarium Chymicum*, reproduced on page 40, represents the death which is part of the alchemical process.

One of Joyce's most striking uses of alchemical processes concerns the cycle of death and rebirth. In a passage about the burial and resurrection of HCE the alchemical processes of inhumation ("inhumationary" 77.33), putrefaction ("portrifaction" 78.21), fermentation ("ferment" 78.27), conjunction (78.35), and circulation ("circulated" 79.04) all appear. After this the hero can "get outside his own length of rainbow trout" (79.07–08) because the rainbow represented the culmination of the alchemical process (see p. 87).

Inhumation, in general the interment of a body, has a specific alchemical meaning; it involves placing a soluble substance in dung in order to dissolve it. Albertus Magnus gives very detailed instructions for this process, including the size of the hole to be dug, the type of dung to be used to fill it,

Illustration 1. The Death of the Alchemical Solar King and Lunar Queen—the sower and the angel blowing the horn herald the resurrection which is to follow. From the *Viridarium Chymicum* of Michaelis Meyeri (Frankfurt, 1688), p. 67. Reprinted by permission of the British Library, London.

and the length of time the substance to be dissolved is to be left.[18] In this passage of *Finnegans Wake* Joyce equates HCE with the substance which undergoes inhumation in order to be reborn as gold: "But abide Zeit's sumonserving, rise afterfall" (78.07).

Putrefaction, as discussed earlier, figures prominently in the death and rebirth symbolism of alchemy,

> The kyllyng Bodyes into corrupcyon forth ledyng,
> And after unto Regeneratyon them ablyng.[19]

Here personified, "portrifaction," unwilling to allow HCE to remain dead, begins to "ramp, ramp, ramp" (78.21) on his grave.

The descriptions of fermentation, a later stage in the alchemical process, are vague and confusing, but it is clear that the Stone was regarded as a ferment, a kind of leaven which "raised" a base metal to its utmost purity, gold. Mystical interpretations of the ferment also abound; George Ripley describes it as a transcendent union of soul and body.[20] Joyce refers to the "ferment," which comes after the putrefaction of the body of HCE, in terms of war; the battle is between earthly and spiritual elements, representing all wars of all time. Fittingly, resolution comes with "conjunction" (78.35), an alchemical process which "was variously defined as the union, or marriage, of male and female, Sun and Moon, agent and patient, form and matter, sulphur and mercury, gross and subtle, fixed and volatile, brother and sister, Hermes' seal and wax, lion and serpent, toad and eagle, the two dragons, etc."[21] Later, while creating his ink, Shem chants "his cantraps of fermented words, abracadabra calubra culorum" (184.26), alchemically, magically, trying to ferment the base ingredients of his work into art. Ripley also lists conjunction as the "Fourth Gate" in his *Compound*, coming before putrefaction; thus, it stands for both the reconciliation of opposites which is the goal of alchemy and also the beginning of the process. Joyce takes advantage of both these aspects in *Finnegans Wake.*

Circulation, a specific alchemical procedure, also implies the circular nature of the entire alchemical work. In *The Fount of Chemical Truth,* Philalethes describes operations which "'circulate' the substance, until the gross is separated from the subtle, and the whole is evenly tempered, the separated elements being then recombined, impregnated, and putrefied."[22] In this passage HCE is "secretly and by suckage feeding on his own misplaced fat" (79.12–13), a circular type of activity which brings to mind the ouroboros, the serpent which devours itself. This symbol for the alchemical work "is the symbol of the circular movement of the alchemical process, consisting of a repeated dissolving, evaporating, and distilling of matter, in which the finer parts ascend and the coarser ones remain in the bottom of the retort."[23] The use of alchemical processes in this passage widens the scope of the burial and resurrection of HCE. Again, Joyce uses alchemy to add another layer of meaning to the text and to exemplify the universality of the death-rebirth theme.

Throughout *Finnegans Wake,* as in the alchemical text the *New Pearl* referred to above, the sons strive to take the place of the father, and any attack on HCE exemplifies the struggle of younger men to usurp the older. This process is always in a sense a rebirth, as the old generation gives way to the new. In regard to the overall structure of *Finnegans Wake,* Ruth Von Phul finds the death-rebirth cycle more important than the Viconian one: "The numerous allusions to Vico should not beguile us into yet one more fruitless attempt to impose a four-part Viconian cycle. This is an older, more familiar cycle, the immemorial, ever-new round of birth, marriage, death and rebirth."[24]

The alchemists often symbolized the resurrection of gold

from a base metal as a phoenix, equating the phoenix with the object of the alchemical work, calling the Stone the "Phoenix of the Sages," and pictorially depicting the success of the alchemical operation as the birth of the phoenix.[25] Although the phoenix is an obvious symbol for rebirth, Joyce specifically relates it to alchemical imagery on several occasions. The mythical bird has a tripartite spirit in *Finnegans Wake* ("the phoenix, his pyre, is still flaming away with trueprattight spirit" 265.08–10) because the alchemists thought of the Stone which it symbolized as a combination of mercury, sulphur, and salt. HCE is referred to as a phoenix (55.28) in a passage about rising and falling, in which "life . . . is a wake" (55.05–06), recalling the death-rebirth symbolism of the song "Finnegan's Wake." In another section in which he is identified with the phoenix HCE appears as the alchemist Paracelsus (see p. 112). We recognize HCE because the initials of the name of the protagonist spell out "Here Comes Everybody": "And with tumblerous legs, redipnominated Helmingham Erchenwyne Rutter Egbert Crumwall Odin Maximus Esme Saxon Esa Vercingetorix Ethelwulf Rupprecht Ydwalla Bentley Osmund Dysart Yggdrasselmann? Holy Saint Eiffel, the very phoenix!" (88.20–24). The first riddle of I.6 also identifies Finn MacCool/HCE with the phoenix (128.35, 136.35).

A passage early in the book specifically describes HCE as the embodiment of the alchemical process:

> He dug in and dug out by the skill of his tilth for himself and all belonging to him and he sweated his crew beneath his auspice for the living and he urned his dread, that dragon volant, and he made louse for us and delivered us to boll weevils amain, that mighty liberator, Unfru-Chikda-Uru-Wukru and begad he did, our ancestor most worshipful, till he thought of a better one in his windower's house with that blushmantle upon him from earsend to earsend. And would again could whispring

> grassies wake him and may again when the fiery bird disembers. And will again if so be sooth by elder to his youngers shall be said. Have you whines for my wedding, did you bring bride and bedding, will you whoop for my deading is a? Wake? *Usqueadbaugham!* (24.03–14)

The alchemical term "dragon volant," the "flying dragon," refers either to mercury alone, or the union of philosophical sulphur and mercury:

> Now, if these two seeds [of philosophical mercury and sulphur], separated one from another, are united spermatically by triumphant Nature, in the book of Mercury, the first mother of metals, the Sages call the substance that results, the flying dragon, because this dragon, being kindled with its fire, in its flight pours abroad into the air fire and a poisonous vapour.[26]

HCE delivers a similar poison, and delivers his people "to boll weevils," but the alchemical process ends with rebirth images in the phoenix, the wedding, and the wake.

The goal of the alchemical process, the Philosopher's Stone, was both a means and an end, a transmuting agent to convert base metals into gold and/or a mystical quintessence which was itself the final goal of the alchemical process. The former view is expressed by an alchemist who holds that the transmuting power is the very essence of the Stone:

> "The true sign by which the Tincture of the physicists is known, is its power of transmuting all imperfect metals into silver (if it be white) or gold (if it be red) if but a small particle of it be injected into a mass of such metals liquefied in a crucible."[27]

The theory arose that the Stone was a medicine, curing metals from their diseased state into their perfect state, gold. Paracelsus states: "'Our Stone is the heavenly and superperfect Medicine, because it washes away all the impurities of metals.'''[28] Extending this concept, some alchemists regarded the Stone as a universal panacea, also capable of curing and perfecting people; in this aspect, the alchemists called it the "elixir."

Finnegans Wake includes the concept of the Stone as elixir. In the "Mime of Mick, Nick, and the Maggies" the flower girls ask a riddle; the proper answer is "heliotrope," but Glugg, in three tries, fails to answer it. The females turn toward Chuff "in heliolatry" (237.01)—since the sun is a symbol for gold, the perfect metal and ultimate aim of the alchemical process, they are here considering Chuff as the Philosopher's Stone. The girls "all alisten to his elixir" (237.08–09), but Chuff cannot provide the panacea; he offers only the comfortable life of a middle-class businessman (235.09–18). Also, as Glasheen points out: "Issy (and seven) is avid for sex, does all she can to rouse the twins; but Shaun [Chuff] is too pure; Shem, though he wills sex, cannot."[29] The girls observe to Chuff, calling him, appropriately, "Stainusless": "Unclean you art not. Outcaste thou are not. Leperstower, the karman's loki, has not blanched at our pollution and your intercourse at ninety legsplits does not defile. . . . You are pure. You are pure. You are in your puerity" (237.21–25). Since the union of male and female is necessary in the alchemical process, such purity or ignorance prevents the achievement of the elixir.

Another allusion to the Stone as elixir occurs in the first riddle, the answer to which is "Finn MacCool." The subject of the riddle "sucks life's eleaxir from the pettipickles of the Jewess" (133.19–20). The sexual is not omitted this time; the secret is obtained in a very direct way from the female, here Mary the Jewess, one of the few women alchemists. Thought to be Miriam, the sister of Moses, she supposedly invented the tribikos, a distilling apparatus with three spouts; the water-bath (still called the *bain-marie* in French); and the kerotakis, an alchemical apparatus that appears in Greek alchemical writing.

"Tincture" was one of the most common names for the Stone; it literally tinctured or tinged a mass of metal in the course of changing it into gold. The concept of the tincture embodies the idea of alchemy as essentially the art of dyeing; its use probably derives from the metal coloring processes of the Egyptian metallurgists, precursors of the alchemists, and from it arose the importance of the color sequence in alchemy. In *Splendor Solis* we read that the tincture "'gives life and colour to all whom it is given to take.'"[30] Some alchemists even regard this tinted gold as better than common gold:

> Zosimos, who lived in the third or fourth century A.D., like the later alchemists of the Middle Ages, seems to have regarded his "tinted", imitative silver and gold as superior in colour and purity to the native metals. Since the tinted gold was yellower than ordinary gold, it was capable of imparting yellowness—or a yellow "seed" or "ferment"—to other metals, thus transmuting them into gold.[31]

The reference to "tincture" (182.09–10) is very appropriate in a passage which emphasizes that Shem's art is "sham" in every imaginable way. He copies the styles of everyone else; his art is "an epical forged cheque . . . for his own private profit" (181.16–17). The passage derides his writing as "pseudostylic shamiana," and accuses him of writing with a "pelagiarist pen" (181.36–182.01, 182.03). Colors also play an important part in this passage, linking Shem the "alshemists's" art to that of the alchemists who sought the Stone by means of color change.

The coming of darkness at the end of the "Mime" includes a reference to the alchemical tincture: "It darkles (tinct, tint) all this our funnaminal world" (244.13). In spite of the darkness, there is some brightness, for this blackness "darkles"; the darkness is just a temporary tint. This is because the night is necessary to bring the day, just as the fall is necessary for resurrection, and just as the blackening, the putrefaction or death of the metal, is necessary for the attainment of the alchemical goal. Specifically, the night is described as the "time of lying together" (244.32), and this, with the reference to the tincture, indicates that a literal sexual act and a metaphorical one (in alchemical terms) will bring the dawn and with it the sun, the symbol of gold and of awakening and life.

Joyce again uses the tincture to express the cyclical nature of reality and the alchemical process in the "Lessons Chapter," where he combines it with other alchemical ideas such as the reconciliation of opposites. With the coming of night in this chapter (276.11–20) comes a consideration of the daily, historical, and cosmic cycles, and an acceptance of them. "We drames our dreams tell Bappy returns. And Sein annews. We will not say it shall not be, this passing of order and order's coming . . ." (277.17–19). One can attempt to escape it, but, paradoxically, the only way to be free of the cycle is to accept it wholeheartedly, or, in the literal terms of the *Wake*, "to chew the cud" (278.02–03). The circular scroll of history contains both praise and tales of impropriety. To all this the left-hand marginal annotation is "*Pitchcap and triangle, noose and tinctunc*" (278.L1). Both pairs juxtapose an instrument of torture with a unifying, reconciling symbol. "Pitchcap" is "a cap lined with pitch, used as an instrument of torture by the soldiery during the Irish rebellion of 1798" (*OED*). The triangle is a symbol of alchemical unity—the mercury, sulphur, and salt thought by Paracelsus to be the constituents of all things are diverse and yet one. The alchemists also equated these three elements with the Blessed Trinity, a profound statement of unity in diversity. However, a triangle is also "a tripod, orig. formed of three halberds stuck in the ground and joined at the top, to which soldiers were formerly bound to be flogged" (*OED*). That Joyce had this meaning of "triangle" in mind is likely, since one of the examples of the use of "pitchcap" given in the *OED* also includes this other instrument of torture: "1842 R. R. Madden *United Irishmen* I.xi 337 The numbers tied up to the triangles and tortured with the scourge, or tormented with the pitchcaps . . . in the year 1798." Thus, "pitchcap and triangle" are opposites and yet the same. "Noose," another torture device, is paired with "tinctunc," the Stone combined with the Tunc page of the Book of Kells. Again, the tincture is a harmonizing agent, turning the chaos and divisiveness of the four elements into a transcendent unity.

The acceptance of the ongoing cycle of human life and history, then, includes both instruments of torture and symbols of ineffable oneness. In alchemical terms, torture, death, and putrefaction of the metal must precede its rebirth as gold; in Christian terms, death must precede rebirth; and in Viconian terms, an age of chaos must come at the end of every cycle and precede the beginning of the new one. Shem's note, light-hearted as it may seem at first glance, concerns the acceptance of the inevitable cycles and the question of unity in diversity, expressed partly in alchemical terms.

Continuing the theme of circularity, Joyce calls the first fall ("initials falls" 286.04) the "primary taincture" (286.05); this sin is the first taint of humanity. Joyce's word "taincture" expresses the *felix culpa* idea so prominent in *Finnegans Wake* since the taint is also the tincture and the stain is the coloring of possible transmutation. Again, redemption requires the taint of sin, the death of the metal.

Alchemists commonly called the Philosopher's Stone the "*lapis*": through this term Joyce expresses several alchemical themes in *Finnegans Wake*. Dolph visualizes the diagram of his mother "in the lazily eye of his lapis, Vieus Von DVbLIn"

(293.11–12). The reference is to: "*Lapis in Via*: stone in the street—the philosophers' stone. *Lapis in Via* von Dublin—philosophers' stone of Dublin. The philosophers' stone is androgynous: it is HCE and ALP. The figure the boys are drawing is the geometrical counterpart of the philosophers' stone."[32] The fact that to begin the process Dolph tells his brother Kev: "First mull a mugfull of mud, son. . . . Anny liffle mud which cometh out of Mam will doob, I guess" (286.35–287.08) testifies that he is leading his brother not only to the secrets of the female but also to the *lapis*. The mud of the Liffey, the excrement of the mother—such are the vile substances in which the alchemists sought the Stone. Also, the connection between the Stone and the landscape of Dublin is fitting, for as the following pages show, the alchemists often associated the *lapis* with the New Jerusalem. As the microcosm, Dublin is the *lapis* which contains all.

Fittingly, the Philosopher's Stone embodies the union of opposites. Philalethes states:

> Our Stone is called a little world, because it contains within itself the active and the passive, the motor and the thing moved, the fixed and the volatile, the mature and the crude—which, being homogeneous, help and perfect each other.[33]

The words, pages, chapters, and *Finnegans Wake* as a whole mirror the all-encompassing nature of the Stone.

Alchemy aimed at bringing about not only the transmutation of metals and the perfection of the human soul, but also the advent of the New Jerusalem. In this paradise the entire earth will be transformed through the spread of alchemy. The author of *An Open Entrance to the Closed Palace of the King* believes that the function of alchemy is to make gold so common that people will no longer worship it; they then will be able to turn their minds to higher things. This "Anonymous Sage and Lover of Truth" states:

> My Book is the precursor of Elias, designed to prepare the Royal way of the Master; and would to God that by its means all men might become adepts in our Art—for then gold, the great idol of mankind, would lose its value, and we should prize it only for its scientific teaching. Virtue would be loved for its own sake.[34]

Michael Sendivogius prophesies a literal new earth, viewing the planet itself as a great distilling vessel which the Creator of all things will form into "a new and more glorious earth" by alchemical processes.[35]

In his *A Suggestive Inquiry Into the Hermetic Mystery,* included in his *Prophecies,* Paracelsus looks forward to the Golden Age, the "'Fourth Monarchy, which is the Intellectual reign of Truth and Peace . . . when abundance of all things by an equitable distribution of all, shall help to break down the competitive barrier of society, and introduce a co-operative alliance among mankind.'" The age is golden because it involves the rediscovery of alchemy and a universal knowledge of the transmutation of metals, but the change will be inner as well as outer. As the translator of the *Prophecies* of Paracelsus states, "Manifestly the Regeneration of the World is treated, occultly the Divine Re-birth in Man may be intended."[36] Paracelsus looked for the salvation and rebirth of the world and of the human soul through alchemy. As *Finnegans Wake* describes this millennium: "Yes, before all this has time to end the golden age must return with its vengeance. Man will become dirigible, Ague will be rejuvenated, woman with her ridiculous white burden will reach by one step sublime incubation . . ." (112.18–21).

This passage involves the way to read *Finnegans Wake.* The text addresses the perplexed reader: "You is feeling like you was lost in the bush, boy? You says: It is a puling sample jungle of woods. You most shouts out: Bethicket me for a stump of a beech if I have the poultriest notions what the farest he all means" (112.03–06). For the golden age, including the interpretation of the *Wake,* we must look to the hen: "Lead, kindly fowl! They always did: ask the ages" (112.09). That is because the hen has no metaphysical or aesthetic views unattached to earth: "she just feels she was kind of born to lay and love eggs" (112.13–14). Many alchemical writers describe the alchemical process in terms of a brooding hen, and sometimes refer to the *vas* in which the process takes place as an egg. Once in the vessel, the *prima materia* was exposed to "a gentle, continuous, airy, vaporous, and well-tempered heat, resembling the degree of warmth with which the hen hatches her eggs."[37] Perhaps the alchemical hen acts as one source for Biddy the hen and her restorative function in *Finnegans Wake.*

In this passage about the way in which to interpret *Finnegans Wake,* "What bird has done yesterday man may do next year" (112.09–10). The hen does what she was born to do, and, as the alchemical allusion shows, unites the literal and symbolic, below and above. The hen's warmth, which hatches the alchemical and literal egg, is natural, is grounded thoroughly in this world, and yet achieves a kind of regeneration as she rescues the letter from the rubbish heap or picks up the pieces after a battle. Again, the physical and spiritual, literal and symbolic function symbiotically. In *Finnegans Wake* eggs and hens often herald the dawn, for example at 613.10–12. However, like the alchemists who use but do not transmute vile substances in their work, the hen does not transcend or remake this world completely—hens lay eggs which become chickens which lay more eggs. Things are not made over completely but merely rearranged: "The awakening is an ambiguous regeneration. . . . Former aspirations and preoccupations return like clothes from the laundry of night . . . ," notes Kenner.[38] In this case the alchemical allusions remind the reader that in *Finnegans Wake* neither the literal nor the symbolic can be ignored at the expense of the other.

In another case an allusion to the German mystical and alchemical writer Jacob Boehme ("behemuth" 244.36) connects the Wakean dawn to the alchemical one. In both, sexual activity leads to dawn: "The time of lying together will come and the wildering of the nicht till cockeedoodle aubens Aurore" (244.32–33). Alchemical texts represent the process as a union of male and female, the achievement of the goal a dawn or resurrection. "Aurore" specifically alludes to Boehme's first book, "Aurora, the Day Spring, or Dawning of the Day in the East, or Morning Redness in the Rising of the Sun." This book, the result of his mystical visions, earned for him persecution from the ecclesiastical authorities, uniting him with the beleaguered HCE in the *Wake*.[39]

The material aspect of the golden age prophesied by alchemy, when all will have enough to eat and the world's goods will be equitably distributed, also functions in the *Wake*: "Hightime is ups be it down into outs according! When there shall be foods for vermin as full as feeds for the fett, eat on earth as there's hot in oven" (239.16–18). Sex will also be freer and open to all equally in the *Wake*'s democratic millennium: "And the world is maidfree" (239.21–22).

MacArthur discusses the theme of the alchemical New Jerusalem in *Finnegans Wake* in terms of Dublin as the Holy City:

> It has been noted (*S*[keleton] *K*[ey], p. 154n) that Dublin is linked to the lapis (293.11–12). This follows a well known alchemical parallel with the Holy City. The same idea occurs at 256.28 where salt is linked to the sign ⊕ which in this context represents Dublin (the General Post Office is central and the Dublin United Tramway Co. form the radii meeting the north and south circular roads). The association of square and circle

> to represent Dublin has also been shown. [By P. Skrabankek, *A Wake Newslitter,* X.2, 22.]
>
> In *Scribbledehobble* appears "Zoetrope, wheel of life, astronomically laid out cities". So at 181.07 "the capital city" is governed in a similar way to the days of the week by the seven planets, Sun, Moon, Mars, Mercury, Jupiter, Venus and Saturn. This idea may come from Campanella or Hermes Trismegistos.
>
> Finally, masculinity (HCE) the sun, city and ⊕ appear as a "blazing urbanorb" at 589.06. Vico speculates that the words urbs and orbis may have a common origin, thus at 140.07 the Dublin motto is altered. (See also 601.05).[40]

Concerning the link of Dublin and a transcendent fourth dimension, Clive Hart says:

> Later (342.17) the sentence "They are at the turn of the fourth of the hurdles" seems to imply that entering the city of Dublin ("Ford-of-Hurdles-Town") is equivalent to entering the "Fourth", that a knowledge of Dublin amounts to an apprehension of Brahman.[41]

This refers not only to a fourth dimension of apprehension, but also to the "Fourth Monarchy" of Paracelsus referred to above.

Other alchemical processes besides those connected with death and rebirth also appear in *Finnegans Wake*. Coagulation appears in a passage in which a jury accuses HCE of numerous crimes, among them incest—"they found him guilty of their and those imputations of fornicolopulation with two of his albowcrural correlations" (557.16–17)—a fitting alchemical accusation, since the union of opposites in the alchemists' work is often depicted as incestuous. They also accuse him of "denying transubstantiation" (557.29) and imploring "on everybody connected with him the curse of coagulation" (557.35–36). Coagulation consists of reducing a liquid to a solid by exposure to heat or air; Philalethes lists it among the last five operations, which result in "purifying the putrefied substance of its dross, by continual ascensions and descents."[42] The charges thus include the denial of Eucharistic transformation and the substitution of an alchemical one. In fact, the jury convicts HCE "be what will of excess his exaltation," a further alchemical process. The purification of coagulation continues "until the dryness gradually thickens the substance, and, finally, under the influence of coction or continued sublimation, induces fixation, the terminal point of which is exaltation, an exaltation which is not local, from the bottom to the surface, but qualitative, from vileness to the highest excellence."[43] The illustration on the following page symbolically depicts the process of exaltation.

The alchemical process of amalgamation exemplifies the theme of opposition and reconciliation so important in the *Wake*; it consists of mixing a precious metal with a base one to make the latter resemble the former. The Canon's Yeoman mentions the process of amalgamation in his tale (l. 771, p. 216). The story of HCE's encounter with the Cad is "an amalgam as absorbing as calzium chloereydes and hydrophobe sponges could make it" (35.01–02). Calcium chloride, a salt which absorbs water from the air, is used as a drying and dehumidifying agent; here it combines with a water-hating sponge. This unlikely amalgam, used to describe the confrontation of HCE with his opposite, the Cad, brings to mind that other Joycean water-lover, Buck Mulligan, who "saved men from drowning" (*U* 4), and his opposite, the hydrophobe Stephen Dedalus.

In sublimation a substance is heated until it vaporizes and rises to the top of the vessel, and is then recondensed back to the bottom of the vessel; consequently, it represents a microcosm of the entire alchemical process, embodying the Hermetic dictum "As above, so below, as below, so above."

Illustration 2. The Enthronement of the King and Queen represents their rebirth and the exaltatio of the alchemical process. From the *Viridarium Chymicum* of Michaelis Meyeri (Frankfurt, 1688), p. 69. Reprinted by permission of the British Library, London.

With a similar world view, Joyce "sublimes" HCE and the rest of the Earwicker family; they are heroic figures, mythic archetypes, and at the same time a unique family of Chapelizod. Sublimation therefore operates within the microcosm-macrocosm theory of alchemy and Jung's view of the "self" to represent the most important literary technique of *Finnegans Wake*. This list of "abusive names he [HCE] was called" (71.05–06) includes "*Sublime Porter*" (72.02–03).

The use of sublimation as a literary technique functions in another passage. The questioners ask a witness: "Happily you were not quite so successful in the process verbal whereby you would sublimate your blepharospasmockical suppressions, it seems?" (515.15–17). "Sublimate" here refers to the psychoanalytic concept whereby a person directs the energy of an impulse from a lower level to a higher, more culturally acceptable one; according to this theory our lowest instincts transform themselves into our highest cultural achievements. Joyce puns on the psychoanalytic and the alchemical meanings of the word; cunningly, he transforms it into a literary technique while simultaneously mocking it. All of *Finnegans Wake* is in a sense a pun on this process—the most mundane matter of life and those elements which we repress are sublimated into art, but at the same time always lead us back to their origins.

In this section the examiners question the witness about the "ballay at the Tailors' Hall" (510.14), that is, what really occurred at HCE's pub on the night in question. The event constantly metamorphoses in Joyce's literary sublimation; it is also the marriage of the Norwegian captain (511.02), Finnegan's wake (the song is echoed at 511.23), a "masked ball" (512.10), a pontifical Mass with excremental overtones (514.27), and "funeral games" (515.23). Similarly, the people present on the occasion and what they did or did not do also change on every line. "As above, so below" state the alchemists—events are both cosmic and mundane; the heroic funeral games are also the drunken scenes at Finnegan's wake.

Sublimation also operates in a passage about the golden age discussed on page 50. The "golden age" to come will be that predicted by Paracelsus, the literal alchemical paradise where material goods are distributed fairly and the spiritual one where people too will be perfected and saved. In the Wakean universe man will become an air-filled dirigible and will literally rise to sublime heights. Woman will reach "sublime incubation"; the eggs upon which she broods will be sublimated, to represent both her physical children and her spiritual ones.

In the *Compound* Ripley regards sublimation as both the spiritualizing of the body and the corporalizing of the spirit, indicating its double movement. He also allies it specifically to the golden age when heaven on earth will be achieved, tying it in with the whole "New Jerusalem" motif of alchemy and Joyce's use of sublimation in *Finnegans Wake.*

> But when these to *Sublymacyon* continuall
> Be laboryd so, wyth hete both moyst and temperate,
> That all ys Whyte and purely made spirituall;
> Than Hevyn uppon Erth must be reitterate,
> Unto the Sowle wyth the Body be reincorporate:
> That Erth becom all that afore was Hevyn,
> Whych wyll be done in *Sublymacyons* sevyn.[44]

Shaun/Kev's marginal comment "*Canine Venus sublimated to Aulidic Aphrodite*" (299.L1) deals with the alchemical process of sublimation as well. Venus has two aspects, Venus Pandemos and Venus Ourania, representing animal love and spiritual love. Joyce expresses this concept by the use of sublimation—the canine, bestial goddess raised to the level of the heavenly, spiritual one by this alchemical process. The "aludel" was the vessel in which the sublimation took place;

thus the "sublimated" Aphrodite is the "aulidic" one. The alchemists regarded the sublimation process with great reverence, finding in it a proof of the theory that the vapors which were produced actually purified the metals.

This note appears in the section in which Dolph reveals to Kev the sexual secrets of the mother, and is the scholarly type of marginal note associated with Shaun/Kev. He sees only the sublimated mother until his brother forces his gaze downward to encompass the earthly mother as well: "But you're holy mooxed and gaping up the wrong palce. . . . You must lap wandret down the bluishing refluction below. Her trunk's not her brainbox" (299.13–19).

Later Shaun will use what he has learned about the female and sublimation in the above passage. The phrase "from the sublime to the ridiculous" (445.27) refers not only to the cliche "It's but one step from the sublime to the ridiculous," but also to the alchemical operation of sublimation. When he makes this statement Shaun has just finished a long, moralistic, high-minded sermon to his sister and the girls of St. Bride's warning them against any and all types of sexual activity, and is about to express his lust for his sister ("Sevenheavens, O heaven! Iy waount yiou!" 446.01–02). At the important transition point between the two comes the reference to sublimation, the process which takes the vile substances of the earth and vaporizes them, but then condenses them back onto the original substance. Ultimately sublimation helped to transform the dross of earth into gold, or at least into something that resembled gold. Shaun hopes to transform his incestuous desires into noble ones in a similar manner.

In the "Courting Interlude" of Shaun's sermon he brags of his capabilities and the deeds he will perform to convince Issy that he is worth loving.[45] Again he uses sublimation to elevate himself (452.14). He says, "I'm the gogetter that'd make it pay like cash registers as sure as there's a pot on a pole. . . .

nothing would stop me for mony makes multimony like the brogues and the kishes. . . . I'd axe the channon and leip a liffey and drink annyblack water that rann onme way" (451.04–15). The "benedictine errand" (452.17) or alchemical transmutation that he will perform is the ultimate heroic deed (see p. 77). He will achieve it, fittingly, on "this night sublime," seated on the three-legged stool of Thrice-Greatest Hermes, and under the aegis of Thoth ("thauthor," "th'other" 452.10, 13).

The alchemical theory that the macrocosm and microcosm reflect each other becomes the basis for a literary technique in *Finnegans Wake,* and such alchemical processes as putrefaction, circulation, and sublimation give Joyce another grounding for the literary technique by which everyday words, characters, and events vaporize into mythic archetypes and cosmic significance and then condense back into jingles, a Chapelizod family, and a not-so-special night in their lives. Joyce finds in alchemy a type of ur-myth which fits his desire to express the most basic themes and cycles of human life, especially that of death and rebirth, which expands from the specific to the general, from the microcosm to the macrocosm, to include the concept of the New Jerusalem. *Finnegans Wake* also reflects the circularity of the alchemical process and its metaphoric death-rebirth level. The text itself is the *vas* or retort in which the author cooks his disparate materials.

Number Symbolism

Many critics have attempted to explain the use of numbers in *Finnegans Wake,* but they function in so many ways that no one schema can adequately account for them. Much of the number symbolism in the book is occult, and, specifically, alchemical. Joyce uses numbers one, two, three, four, and ten alchemically in the *Wake*; they operate in the texture and structure of the work, on both the microcosmic and macrocosmic levels. Ultimately they lead to and explain the problem of "circling the square" and they indicate that Joyce meant *Finnegans Wake* itself to be the solution to this problem and the equivalent of the Philosopher's Stone.

The "axiom of Maria" expresses the importance of these numbers in alchemy. It runs: "One becomes two, two becomes three, and out of the third comes the one as the fourth."[1] This also demonstrates the cyclical nature of the process, for one and four, at opposite ends of the work, are yet the same; they are both the beginning and the end. Because of this, the process can run either way; four becomes one just as one becomes four. Jung describes the alchemical process as follows:

> It begins with the four separate elements, the state of chaos, and ascends by degrees to the three manifestations of Mercurius in

> the inorganic, organic, and spiritual worlds; and, after attaining the form of Sol and Luna (i.e., the precious metals gold and silver, but also the radiance of the gods who can overcome the strife of the elements by love), it culminates in the one and indivisible (incorruptible, ethereal, eternal) nature of the *anima,* the *quinta essentia, aqua permanens,* tincture, or *lapis philosophorum.* This progression from the number 4 to 3 to 2 to 1 is the "axiom of Maria," which runs in various forms through the whole of alchemy like a *leitmotiv.*[2]

The four at the beginning of the alchemical process are usually considered to be the four elements, although they also represent the four seasons, the four directions, and sometimes the four qualities (attractive, retentive, digestive, expulsive), as in the frontispiece to Ripley's *Compound of Alchymie* in *Theatrum Chemicum Brittanicum.* In that illustration, which claims: "Here followeth the Figure conteyning all / the secrets of the Treatise both great & small," these groupings of four enclose a circle which explains the Great Work.[3] In the form of a square they symbolize chaos, division, and fragmentation, the square pictorially depicting the most extreme representation of separation possible. Alchemical literature and pictorial symbolism abound in such examples: earth, air, fire, and water form the corners of a square surrounding a representation of the alchemical work in an illustration from *The Hermetic Museum.*[4] Since alchemists believed that the four elements composed all things, they naturally began the Great Work, perhaps both literally and metaphorically, with them. However, they then had to account for the production of three philosophical principles of all things from these four physical elements; they believed that the elements acting on each other produced mercury, sulphur, and salt:

> The three Principles of things are produced out of the four elements in the following manner: Nature, whose power is in her obedience to the Will of God, ordained from the very

> beginning, that the four elements should incessantly act on one another, so, in obedience to her behest, fire began to act on air, and produced Sulphur; air acted on water and produced Mercury; water, by its action on earth, produced Salt. Earth, alone, having nothing to act upon, did not produce anything, but became the nurse, or womb, of these three Principles.[5]

The alchemical workers regarded these principles as spiritual qualities rather than physical entities; the alchemical process itself moves from physical to spiritual.

While the four elements gave rise to the three principles in alchemy, the number three has importance in and of itself as well. Rather than dwell on the means by which four become three become two become one, some alchemists regard the three as constituents of the Stone and emphasize the fact that they are three and yet one. Basilius Valentinus states:

> . . . the root of philosophic sulphur, which is a heavenly spirit, is united in the same material with the root of the spiritual and supernatural mercury, and the principle of spiritual salt—out of which is made the Stone, and not out of several things. That universal thing, the greatest treasure of earthly wisdom, is one thing, and the principles of three things are found in one, which has power to change all metals into one.[6]

As the above indicates, there is some vacillation in alchemy between four and three. Is the Stone composed of four elements or three principles? Jung states that "the uncertainty as to three or four amounts to a wavering between the spiritual and the physical,"[7] which relates to the traditions of esoteric and exoteric alchemy previously discussed. Some texts make a distinction between the two while others regard them as inseparable. In any case, the history of alchemy encompasses both aspects, that it was a spiritual process concerned with the perfection of the human soul and a chemical process concerned with the transmutation of base metals into gold.

All of these ideas find expression in *Finnegans Wake*. The four elements appear often, for example at 127.05–06,

132.07–08, 172.18–20, 255.05–12, 280.34–35, 469.03–04. Although they are not explicitly alchemical, an examination of the contexts in which they appear clearly shows that they are part of the alchemical *leitmotif*. Three of them refer to the chaos and destruction symbolized by the four elements in alchemy. In the first question in I.6 at 127.05–06, the subject of the riddle is tortured by the use of the four elements—he is buried, burned, drowned, and hanged. The passage at 172.18–20 describes four ways in which Shem would not commit suicide, all explicitly related to earth, air, fire, and water. A more universal destruction through the four elements occurs on 255.05–12—a dead man lies in the earth, his dust mingling with the dust of the ages; storks abandon the nests of eagles; a fiery depth charge destroys its target; and a flood destroys the entire earth. The other references indicate the opposite aspect of the four elements, for although they represent division and chaos at the beginning of the alchemical process, they also stand for its end, the reconciliation which comes with the achievement of the *lapis*. In the division lies the potential unity. For example, on 132.07–08, again in the first question of the "Riddles Chapter," Finn MacCool includes all four elements in a more positive way; the alliteration gives a feeling of oneness between him and his environment. Symbols of peace and rest characterize the use of the four elements on 280.34–35: "Sleep in the water, drug at the fire, shake the dust off and dream your one who would give her sidecurls to." These references suggest the possibilities of transcendence inherent in the four elements. In III.2, "Jaun Before St. Bride's," Shaun also uses the four elements in a positive way. As he is taking leave of the girls on 469.03–04, he suggests the good things he expects to encounter on his journey in terms of earth, fire, air, and water.

In *Finnegans Wake* four occurs primarily as the four old men, who have a multitude of identities. Campbell and Robinson describe some of them:

> The four Evangelists coalesce with four Irish annalists, whose chronicle of ancient times is known as *The Book of the Four Masters*. These four again coalesce with four old men, familiars to the tavern of HCE, who forever sit around fatuously rechewing tales of the good old days. These four guardians of ancient tradition are identical with the four "World Guardians" (*Lokapālas*) of the Tibetan Buddhistic mandalas, who protect the four corners of the world—these being finally identical with the four caryatids, giants, dwarfs, or elephants, which hold up the four corners of the heavens.[8]

When the four act in their guise of the Evangelists, one of their most common identities in *Finnegans Wake,* they are tied closely to alchemical symbolism, for some alchemical illustrations represent the diverse elements of the beginning of the process as the four Evangelists. Roland McHugh shows that in the Buffalo Notebooks Joyce makes a similar association, linking Matthew, Mark, Luke, and John to the four directions, the four elements, and the four qualities which make up those elements, cold, warm, moist, and dry.[9] The weather report for a day on which "our lord of the heights" and "our lady of the valley" (501.30) have an assignation includes these four qualities (502.18–19). "Calid," warm, serves a double function; the *Sophic Hydrolith* names this early alchemist in a list of "some of the true Sages (besides those named in Holy Scripture) who really knew this Art."[10] In *Finnegans Wake,* the four represent the four directions in at least one appearance: "a northern tory, a southern whig, an eastanglian chronicler and a landwester guardian" (42.28–29). On 223.29–33 the four Evangelists are explicitly identified with the four elements.

The four old men in *Finnegans Wake* represent a square or a rectangle, for example when they act as the bedposts of HCE and ALP's bed (555.07–11), to indicate that they, like the square formed by the four elements in alchemical symbolism, are as widely separated and divergent from each other as possible. Their positions at the bedposts give the four different points of view in III.4, and as "the four maaster waves of Erin" (384.06) they give four separate versions of the Tristan and Iseult story. Also, when they arrive to question the recumbent Yawn in III.3 they think of how they will spread "in quadriliberal their azurespotted fine attractable nets" (477.19–20) over him by standing at the four corners surrounding him and spreading the net from one to another.

Three has importance in *Finnegans Wake* as it does in alchemy. As a grouping of characters, three appears most often as the three soldiers who witness HCE's sin in the Park. This group of three can be said to be a form of or derived from the four as they are in alchemy—the three soldiers constitute an aspect of the observing, questioning, jury function of the four.

Like the alchemical triad, that of *Finnegans Wake* often represents the idea of the trinity, of three-in-one. MacArthur has explicated a number of alchemical triads in the *Wake* which are composed of opposites and their combination, showing how important the theme is in the book.[11] Aside from the specific alchemical references, however, the theme of the trinity in *Finnegans Wake* has many analogies to the alchemical system, primarily the idea of unity in diversity. The questioning of Yawn in III.3 leads to the revelation that he is one with his brother and together they are one with their father.

> —*Three in one, one and three.*
> ——*Shem and Shaun and the shame that sunders em.*
> ——*Wisdom's son, folly's brother.* (526.13–15)

Yawn's reply to an earlier question leaves no doubt that HCE and his sons are analogous to the alchemical and Christian trinity:

—Are you in your fatherick, lonely one?
—The same. Three persons. (478.28–29)

A version of the letter says of HCE, "There were three men in him" (113.14).

Margaret Solomon asserts greater importance for the number three in *Finnegans Wake,* one which has structural implications. She interprets the tale of the Norwegian captain and the tailor as "the union of the three into one" and interprets the homosexual activity in the story of Buckley and the Russian General as a trinity in which the sons unite with the father. Solomon goes farther, claiming that the book itself forms a tripartite pattern:

> The Prankquean story, then, though not strictly a generating episode, can be regarded as the prime example of a tripartite pattern which is not only repeated again and again but which, with the addition of the Viconian *ricorso,* comprises the total structure of the *Wake.*[12]

As in alchemy, three in *Finnegans Wake* can be generated by four, a step in the process by which the four become the one, or the goal in itself, a trinity which is a unity.

Just as there is a wavering between four and three in alchemy, so there is in *Finnegans Wake.* As Clive Hart points out:

> Throughout *Finnegans Wake,* in fact, it is very often possible to group a series of symbols, phrases, or people into either a three-part or a four-part configuration, depending on our point of view. There are three children, but Isolde has a double, making a fourth; the four evangelists each have a house, but one of them is invisible since it is no more than a point in space (367.27).[13]

Also, Johnny always lags behind, often leaving the four old men only a threesome:

First klettered Shanator Gregory, seeking spoor through the deep timefield, Shanator Lyons, trailing the wavy line of his partition footsteps (something in his blisters was telling him all along how he had been in that place one time), then his Recordership, Dr Shunadure Tarpey, caperchasing after honourable sleep, hot on to the aniseed and, up out of his prompt corner, old Shunny MacShunny, MacDougal the hiker, in the rere of them on the run, to make a quorum. (475.23–31)

The four become three in another way, when three of the Evangelists join together to form the Synoptic Gospels, leaving out the fourth. "And, since threestory sorratelling was much too many, they maddened and they morgued and they lungd and they jowld. Synopticked on the word" (367.15–17). In this way the four become three, the three become two (two gospels, the Synoptic Gospel and John), and the two become one (the two gospels relate one life, the life of Christ). The movement here is alchemical.

A reference to *De signatura salium* . . . ("signs on the salt" 393.02), a treatise by the seventeenth-century German chemist and alchemist Johann Rudolph Glauber, also exemplifies how four become one. The four old men, Matt Gregory, Marcus Lyons, Luke Tarpey, and Johnny MacDougall, each supply a version of the Tristan and Iseult story in this chapter. Glauber's work shows how four diverse interpretations can be reconciled into one: "According to this, the original sign for salt was ⊡, which associates it with the lapis."[14] In the alchemical work the square, representing chaos, becomes a circle, symbol of unity; the four elements are reconciled into the unity of the *lapis*. Here the chaos of the four old men's ramblings form one tale.

Clive Hart interprets the structure and meaning of *Finnegans Wake* from this alternation between three and four. In his view, Joyce uses both a 3+1 Viconian scheme and a 4+1 quasi-Indian scheme in the overall structure of the book:

> By squeezing four cycles into three Joyce is, so to speak, superimposing a square on a triangle and so constructing Aristotle's symbol for the body and soul unified in a single being. The implication seems to be that in *Finnegans Wake* we may find a complete and balanced cosmos in which spirit informs and enhances the gross matter represented by the four elements; Joyce could hardly have made a more ambitious symbolic claim for his book.[15]

Joyce is also constructing a symbol for the Great Work by his use of three and four. In an emblem for the alchemical work from the *Viridarium Chymicum* a man and woman lean on a circle representing the earth, within which is a triangle which encloses a square. In another illustration from that work, chaos surrounds a square representing the four seasons, within which is a triangle.[16]

The attempt to find a "complete and balanced cosmos" including both spirit and body also derives from alchemy; the alchemical process refines the chaos and physicality of the four elements into harmony and spirituality. In fact, alchemy is an encompassing symbol for such a process and for the union of opposites it represents. Joyce's desire to create a work of art that contains both body and spirit reflects, as we have seen, his view of art and the artist, a view that is illuminated by his use of alchemy.

Two, like three, is an important step in the alchemical process and also represents an important aspect of the art in its own right.

> Whoever would be a student of this sacred science must know the marks whereby these three Principles are to be recognized, and also the process by which they are developed. For as the three Principles are produced out of four, so they, in their turn, must produce two, a male and a female; and these two must produce an incorruptible one, in which are exhibited the four (elements) in a highly purified and digested condition, and with their mutual strife hushed in unending peace and good-will.[17]

As this indicates, alchemical texts most often regarded the two as male and female, their union a sexual one. This male-female duality is one of the most prominent in the Hermetic Art. The author of *The Golden Tract* counsels: "Know that the secret of the work consists in male and female, *i.e.,* an active and a passive principle," and asks, "When was there placed before your eyes the idea of most fervent love, the male and the female embracing each other so closely that they could no more be torn asunder, but through unsearchable love become *one*?"[18]

The two substances which unite are often considered gold and silver, usually represented pictorially as the sun and the moon or personified as the Solar King and the Lunar Queen. One text states: "Sun and Moon must have intercourse, like that of a man and woman: otherwise the object of our Art cannot be attained. All other teaching is false and erroneous."[19] Numerous pictorial representations show the union of the Solar King and the Lunar Queen; the series of pictures in the *Rosarium Philosophorum* graphically illustrates the Royal Marriage in all its stages, from holding hands to the sexual act to the creation of a hermaphrodite.

This union of male and female came to symbolize the entire process of the production of the *lapis,* "since, as a mythologem, it expresses the archetype of the union of opposites."[20] The texts often portray these opposites as brother and sister; as Jung explains: "The brother-sister pair stands allegorically for the whole conception of opposites. These have a wide range of variation: dry-moist, hot-cold, male-female, sun-moon, gold-silver, mercury-sulphur, round-square, water-fire, volatile-solid, physical-spiritual, and so on."[21] The Royal Marriage of the alchemical process becomes, then, incestuous. At the end of *The Golden Tract* the author gives a parable which supposedly reveals the secret of the Hermetic Art. In it he guards a chamber in which a brother and sister have been imprisoned for the crime of incest. Left alone in the cell, the two unite, then die; their bodies putrefy in the sealed chamber. After an interval, they arise as King and Queen, their resurrection being accompanied by riches, the renewal and restoration of youth, and a panacea for all diseases.[22] Jung interprets the fact that the King and Queen in the *Rosarium Philosophorum* have joined their left hands as an indication that the union is somehow dangerous and illicit, "that the desired *coniunctio* was not a legitimate union but was always—one could almost say, on principle—incestuous."[23] For Jung this too is part of the process of individuation: "Whenever this drive for wholeness appears, it begins by disguising itself under the symbolism of incest, for, unless he seeks it in himself, a man's nearest feminine counterpart is to be found in his mother, sister, or daughter."[24] When the patient in therapy projects his infantile fantasies onto the doctor, the latter replaces the members of the patient's family, making the psychoanalytic process also incestuous. In modern psychological terms, incest stands for the union of conscious and unconscious essential to the process of individuation.

The use of alchemy and incest in *Finnegans Wake* also indicates Joyce's belief that art should express a complete cosmos. In its truest sense, Jung believes, alchemy is a physical attempt to redeem matter and people that is complementary to a spiritual Christian redemption.

> Here again [in the incest motif] we see the contrast between alchemy and the prevailing Christian ideal of attempting to restore the original state of innocence by monasticism and, later, by the celibacy of the priesthood. The conflict between worldliness and spirituality, latent in the love-myth of Mother and Son, was elevated by Christianity to the mystic marriage of sponsus (Christ) and sponsa (Church), whereas the alchemists transposed it to the physical plane as the coniunctio of Sol and

> Luna. The Christian solution of the conflict is purely pneumatic, the physical relations of the sexes being turned into an allegory or—quite illegitimately—into a sin that perpetuates and even intensifies the original one in the Garden. Alchemy, on the other hand, exalted the most heinous transgression of the law, namely incest, into a symbol of the union of opposites, hoping in this way to bring back the golden age. For both trends the solution lay in extrapolating the union of sexes into another medium: the one projected it into the spirit, the other into matter.[25]

Thus, neither alchemy which worked only on the physical level nor Christianity deals with both upper and lower, with the kind of psychic integration that Jung feels is necessary to achieve selfhood. Alchemy attempted to deal with this, but the attempt was, according to Jung, merely compensatory, called forth by a masculine, spiritual Christianity. Joyce, however, successfully combines alchemy and Christianity, transmutation and transubstantiation, physical and spiritual.

The alchemists often represented the result of the union as the conception and birth of a child, and sometimes called the Stone the *filius philosophorum.* The *vas,* the vessel in which the union took place, was "a kind of matrix or uterus from which the *filius philosophorum,* the miraculous stone, is to be born."[26] The *Compound of Alchymie* instructs the alchemist to "Close up the matryce and norysh the seed" after the conjunction takes place; then, several months later, the worker must open the vessel "and fede the chyld whych ys then ybore / with mylk and mete ay more and more." Some texts symbolize the fruit of the alchemical union as a hermaphrodite or what they called the alchemical rebis, "the word *rebis* in Alchemy always referring to the bisexual, that is to the perfectly balanced individual."[27] The *Rosarium Philosophorum* contains several representations of the hermaphrodite born of the union of King and Queen (illustrations 8, 11, 12, 13, 14, 15).

From this representation of the end of alchemy as the birth of a child springs the emphasis on the doctrine that in alchemy two become one. This symbolizes the ultimate alchemical mystery, that opposites unite, restoring primal unity. A. E. Waite explores the spiritual level of this aspect of alchemy, tying it into the "golden age" motif discussed earlier:

> Those Hermetic texts which bear a spiritual interpretation and are as if a record of spiritual experience present, like the literature of physical alchemy, the following aspects of symbolism: (a) the marriage of sun and moon; (b) of a mystical king and queen; (c) an union between natures which are one at the root but diverse in manifestation; (d) a transmutation which follows this union and an abiding glory therein. It is ever a conjunction between male and female in a mystical sense; it is ever the bringing together by art of things separated by an imperfect order of things; it is ever the perfection of nature by means of this conjunction. But if the mystical work of alchemy is an inward work in consciousness, then the union between male and female is an union in consciousness, and if we remember the tradition of a state when male and female had not as yet been divided, it may dawn upon us that the higher alchemy was a practice for the return into this ineffable mode of being. The traditional doctrine is set forth in the *Zohar* and it is found in writers like Jacob Boehme; it is intimated in the early chapters of Genesis and, according to an apocryphal saying of Christ, the kingdom of heaven will be manifested when two shall be as one, or where that state has been once again attained.[28]

The number two also figures prominently in *Finnegans Wake.* Like the alchemical two, it arises out of the three but has significance of its own. The primary manifestation of two in *Finnegans Wake,* the twins Shem and Shaun, issues out of the three soldiers who spy on HCE in the Park. When they unite to overthrow the father, Shem and Shaun act as outgrowths of the hostile, spying, antagonistic soldiers. One of the many attempts to describe the sin of HCE refers to this relationship between three and two:

> Thus the unfacts, did we possess them, are too imprecisely few to warrant our certitude, the evidencegivers by legpoll too untrustworthily irreperible where his adjugers are semmingly freak threes but his judicandees plainly minus twos. (57.16–19)

Like the alchemical two, the warring brothers in the *Wake,* completely different in habits and character, do not remain in opposition. At times, Yawn admits, he feels "that I'm not meself at all, no jolly fear, when I realise bimiselves how becomingly I to be going to become" (487.18–19). At 563.37 the twins Jerry and Kevin become "kerryjevin," a complete mingling of identities.

Some specifically alchemical pairs of antagonistic rivals also fight and "reamalgamerge" in the *Wake.* In a passage in which Yawn, by answering to the charge of plagiarism, has already switched roles with his brother, he calls on Avicenna ("avicendas," "Ibn Sen" 488.06–07) as well as Bruno of Nola. The two names of this eleventh-century Arabian alchemist, Avicenna and Ibn Sen, manifest his split personality: he "was a drunkard and yet controlled numberless legions of spirits."[29] Avicenna also represents the inner division experienced by Yeats and personified by Michael Robartes and Owen Aherne. As the narrator of "Rosa Alchemica" struggles against the influence of Robartes, he hears a distant voice saying, "'Our master Avicenna has written that all life proceeds out of corruption.'"[30]

Avicenna, an authority on medicine, was regarded with great reverence in medieval times. The sixteenth-century alchemist and physician Paracelsus, espousing a medicine based on experiment rather than authority, threw Avicenna's *Canon* into the St. John's Day celebration bonfire in Basel.[31]

In this passage concerned with Bruno's notion of the identity of opposites, Paracelsus and Avicenna become another warring pair who are yet reflections of one identity.

Paracelsus also burned the works of Galen, another ancient medical authority. Atherton notes that in using the word "lithargogalenu" (184.13) Joyce might either be "considering Galen as an Alchemist or referring to the public burning of his works by Paracelsus. But Alchemy certainly comes into the passage."[32] (For the full alchemical context of the passage, see pp. 131–33.) Another reference to Galen occurs as Shaun reviles his brother: "Then he went to Cecilia's treat on his solo to pick up Galen" (424.07). Shaun, ridiculing Shem for studying Galen, acts as Paracelsus in this passage, whereas in the passage on 488 just discussed he identifies with Paracelsus' foe Avicenna. The "Ex. Ex. Ex. Ex." (424.13) which ends the attack could either be a stutterer's attempt at "excommunicated" or the kisses at the end of a letter. Paracelsus and Galen, Shem and Shaun, all pairs of opposites exist in a tenuous balance of love and hate, attraction and repulsion, opposition and unity.

An alchemical reference enters into another passage about the relationship between the two brothers. "Signed with the same salt" (168.08) refers to Glauber's treatise on his *sal mirabile, De signatura salium. . . .*[33] The question concerns unity in diversity, or diversity in unity. Antonius has completed a triangle with Burrus and Caseous the page before (167.01–04), a base and an acid have combined to form a salt (167.19–22), and here Shaun disassociates himself from his brother by asserting the link between them: "were he my own breastbrother, my doubled withd love and my singlebiassed hate, were we bread by the same fire and signed with the same salt. . . ." Glauber's salt, the universal solvent, reduced all things to a liquid primary matter preparatory to converting them into gold. Thus, the brothers, although different in manifestation, have the same primary matter underneath.

Hermes, the supposed founder of the Hermetic Art, and Thoth, his Egyptian counterpart, constitute another brotherly set of opposites in *Finnegans Wake.* Hermes lurks around most of the allusions to Thoth—the Egyptian god is "that halpbrother of a herm" (66.26), "thother brother" (224.33). As these references show, Joyce plays on the name "Thoth" and its affinity with "other"; Hart suggests that Joyce derived the Same-Other polarity from Plato's *Timaeus* by way of Yeats' *A Vision.*[34] In any case, it operates throughout the *Wake* in this regard: Thoth is "tother" (143.19) and "th'other" (452.13); he is "totether" (413.27); his is the "hother prace" (350.19) or "toth's tother's place" (570.13). Thoth represents, then, both unity and difference. Joyce reinforces this identification linguistically; on several occasions the god's name stretches over two words, as in "tho' th'" (238.08), "th'osirian" (350.25) (Thoth and Osiris were brothers; Thoth became scribe to Osiris), and "Call'st thou? Think" (442.19–20).

The male-female union has importance in *Finnegans Wake* as well; HCE and ALP are a universal couple, as is the alchemical one. MacArthur states that the union of opposites, so important to alchemy and Jungian psychology, may have been derived from many sources by Joyce, but he also states that in *Finnegans Wake* this union specifically "finds expression in the idea of the conjunction of male and female, chymical wedding, Adam ○ and Eve □, rex and regina, gold and silver, etc. (104.09, 222.18, 251.12, 260.16, 275.15, 284.10, 305.L1, 366.11, 585.22, to mention a few.)"[35] Joyce explicitly relates HCE and ALP to the sun and the moon in Buffalo Notebook 35, where he equates the sign for HCE, ⊓⊓, to Sol, and that for ALP, △, to Luna.[36] This association manifests itself on 202.26–32, where the "happy fault" committed by HCE and ALP involves the sun and moon. Joyce's use of the alchemical symbols of the sun and the moon also make HCE and ALP the Solar King and Lunar Queen (for example, 202.26–30, where the action is definitely sexual).

Besides the large mergings of characters into each other, hundreds of examples of the union of opposites enrich the texture of *Finnegans Wake,* many connected with chemistry or alchemy. For instance, "an amalgam as absorbing as calzium chloereydes and hydrophobe sponges could make it" (35.01–02) combines a water absorber with a water hater (see p. 54). "Ashreborn" (59.18), besides being one of the opposites which goes into the formation of a salt, also combines within itself the idea of death by fire and rebirth, and therefore the phoenix, symbol for the culmination of the alchemical process. "Another chemical phrase 'lead's plumbate' (541.23) contains a positive form of lead compounded with a negative form."[37] Of course, Joyce had many sources for the union of opposites, but clearly alchemy was among them.

The incest theme in *Finnegans Wake* most often concerns HCE's desires for his daughter Isabel. As the supposedly dead Tim Finnegan he stirs when the mourners at his wake discuss the two aspects of his daughter, the pure and the sensuous (27.11–24). HCE admits his feelings to the customers in the tavern: "I reveal thus my deepseep daughter which was bourne up pridely out of medsdreams unclouthed when I was pillowing in my brime" (366.13–15), and ALP understands that her "sonhusband" is turning away from her for a "daughterwife" (627.01–02). The father usually represses his sexual desires for his daughter, though, veiling them in literary or mythic stories such as Tristan and Iseult; such substitution is consonant with the Jungian theory that the desire for wholeness represented by incest frightens us and that we therefore bury it in our unconscious minds. HCE's guilt could have been relieved somewhat had he read any of the alchemical texts in which an incestuous act restores fruitfulness to a sterile land.[38]

Unlike HCE, Shaun quite brazenly flaunts his feelings for

his sister at times, particularly in III.2. As Jaun, he "made out through his eroscope the apparition of his fond sister Izzy for he knowed his love by her waves of splabashing and she showed him proof by her way of blabushing nor could he forget her so tarnelly easy as all that since he was brotherbesides her benedict godfather" (431.14–18). Jaun's overtures to Izzy here show a more than brotherly affection. As her "benedict godfather," he becomes Basilius Valentinus, author of several alchemical texts. "I, Basil Valentine, brother of the Benedictine Order, do testify that I have written this book," states the author of the *Twelve Keys,* a work which represents the alchemical process in terms of brother/sister incest.[39] In his sermon he suggests that Izzy "love through the usual channels, cisternbrothelly" (436.14), indicating both his Machiavellian attempts to gain his end and perhaps an unconscious understanding that psychologically incest represents a desire for wholeness. The alchemical conjunction of red and white appears in another incestuous passage: Shaun tells his sister, "I'd be staggering humanity and loyally rolling you over, my sowwhite sponse, in my tons of red clover" (451.19–21). Alchemy again reveals Jaun's true desires on 452.08–19 when he employs allusions to Thoth, sublimation, and ether to seduce his sister.

The appearance of the hermaphrodite in *Finnegans Wake* also exemplifies the union of opposites and the use of alchemical imagery. The trial chapter, I.3, begins with a reference to HCE's ambiguous sexuality: "you spoof of visibility in a freakfog, of mixed sex cases among goats" (48.01–02). The chapter continues with many other allusions to such sexual confusion, as in the references to "his husband" (49.02) and "her wife Langley" (50.06); clearly both HCE and ALP encompass both male and female. Also, HCE's sin in the Park, mysterious as it remains in spite of all the talk about it, involves both homosexual and heterosexual acts:

> Supposing, for an ethical fict, him, which the findings showed, to have taken his epscene licence before the norsect's divisional respectively as regards them male privates and or concomitantly with all common or neuter respects to them public exess females . . . (523.33–524.01).

He has sinned against the bylaws of both the "sparkers' and succers' amusements section of our beloved naturpark" (524.05–06), says one witness, while HCE, transformed into Mr. Coppinger, answers the accusation by "touching what the good book says of toooldaisymen, concerning the merits of early bisectualism" (524.11–12). That this refers to HCE as alchemical hermaphrodite or rebis is clearly demonstrated by the fact that the whole passage occurs in response to the need for a rebus in order to understand the story: "—Perhaps you can explain, sagobean? The Mod needs a rebus" (523.19–20).

Just as the alchemical process ends with a birth, so does the artistic one. *Finnegans Wake* is the *lapis,* the result of the union of four, three, two, and one, the container of all opposites, the intersection of the eternal and universal with the temporal and particular.

The alchemical process ends in an all-inclusive unity, a harmony that proceeds from chaos and the reconciliation of warring elements. The "axiom of Maria," a statement of the movement of the process from four to three to two to one, expresses this unity, imaged in the perfect number ten, the sum of these numbers. Campbell and Robinson explain the importance of ten in cabalistic theory:

> In the cabalistic texts, the Creator is spoken of as "Ainsoph." He is represented by the number One. The movement of this Power toward Queen Zero, his bride, generates the numbers from two to nine, and his ultimate union with her, in the number ten, 1–0, initiates a new decade.[40]

Ten also represents the Philosopher's Stone.[41] Joyce specifically uses these cabalistic and alchemical meanings of the number ten in *Finnegans Wake*: "Ainsoph, this upright one, with that noughty besighed him zeroine. To see in his horrorscup he is mehrkurios than saltz of sulphur" (261.23–26). Mercury, sulphur, and salt composed the alchemical triad which formed the *lapis*; here Joyce equates the ten formed by Ainsoph and his wife to the alchemical goal.

The numbers in the *Wake* lead to another consideration—the problem of squaring the circle. One of the so-called unsolved problems of antiquity, squaring the circle involves constructing a square equal in area to a given circle using only a straightedge and a compass; calculating the exact value of π is therefore an important aspect of the problem. Over the centuries hundreds of people have attempted its solution, sometimes seriously, sometimes ludicrously. Weary of scrutinizing the results of these attempts, the *Académie Française* passed a resolution in 1775 not to examine any more solutions. Still, the circle squarers continued; the Indiana Legislature nearly passed a bill in 1897 legislating the value of π and accepting it as a gift to the state from a man who claimed to have squared the circle.[42] Nicholas of Cusa, who appears in *Finnegans Wake,* worked on the problem, while Leopold Bloom hoped to win the government premium of £1,000,000 sterling by its solution (*U* 718).

Bloom in 1904 need not bother any longer, however, for in 1882 Lindemann solved the problem by proving that it could not be solved since π is a transcendental number.[43] Perhaps this mathematical "solution" to the problem, that it couldn't be done, in the year of his birth prompted Joyce to investigate the problem artistically. There was literary precedent; at the end of the *Paradiso* Dante uses squaring the circle as an image for the impossibility of expressing in words his vision of the divine (Canto XXXIII, 11.133–37).[44] In the "Lessons Chapter" of *Finnegans Wake,* the marginal comment to "All the charictures in the drame!" is "ALL SQUARE" (302.31–32, R2).[45] But Joyce most clearly expresses the feeling that he was coming to grips with a similar problem in the *Wake* in a mock/serious letter he wrote to Harriet Shaw Weaver when she was trying to guess the name of his Work in Progress:

> I am making an engine with only one wheel. No spokes of course. The wheel is a perfect square. You see what I am driving at, don't you. I am awfully solemn about it, mind you, so you must not think it is a silly story about the mouse and the grapes. No, it's a wheel, I tell the world. *And* it's all *square*. (*Letters I*, 251)

Alchemy, regarded for most of its history as the illicit, left-hand path to knowledge, reversed this ancient mathematical problem; the alchemical process is, in effect, a metaphoric solution to the problem of circling the square. The four elements in their original chaotic state eventually combine in a higher unity; in their uncombined state they represent a square, combined a circle, leading to the many squares and circles in representations of the alchemical work. Emblem XXI in *Atalanta Fugiens* shows an alchemist drawing a circle, inside of which is a triangle, which encloses a square containing a circle with a naked man and woman. The motto to this illustration reads:

> Make a circle out of a man and a woman, out
> of this a square, out of this a triangle,
> make a circle and you will have the Philosophers'
> Stone.[46]

Of the Great Work, Ripley states: "And of the Quadrangle make ye a Figure round, / Then have ye honie of our bene hive."[47] Although it has several other origins, including Joyce's assertion that its source is Euclid (*Letters I*, 242), the geometrical diagram on 293 may also derive partially from alchemy. Arguing that Joyce opposed the thinking of Yeats and others, who work up elaborate webs of relationships until they lose sight of any connection to earth, Hugh Kenner states:

> Joyce, always interested in the popular parodies of great traditions, put this component of his Dublin's clumsy intellectualism to delighted use. In the geometry-lesson in *Finnegans Wake,* Dolph performs for the scandalized Kev a lewd grammatical exegesis of a diagram strikingly like the alchemical formula quoted by Jung: "Fac de masculo et foemina circulum rotundum, et de eo extrahe quadrangulum et ex quadrangulo triangulum; fac circulum rotundum (of the triangle) et habebis lapidum Philosophorum." [Jung, *Integration of the Personality,* p. 145] Joyce's diagram is based on the construction for an equilateral triangle (Delta=ALP), and all the secrets of the universe are extracted from it, F 293. Allegory gets out of control the moment we cease to *see* the relationships and start walking blindfold a logical plank.[48]

Consistently in his work Joyce satirizes those who flee from the world into an abstract intellectual realm; his use of alchemy aids these parodies.

The symbolism of circling the square carries over into the alchemical equipment—the vessel or *vas* is round not just to imitate the womb, but also to signify its philosophic aspect. Jung states: "This basin . . . is circular, because it is the matrix of the perfect form into which the square, as an imperfect form, must be changed. In the square the elements are still separate and hostile to one another and must therefore be united in the circle."[49] "Circling the square" appears directly after the section in *Finnegans Wake* in which Shem alchemically makes ink out of his own excrement (186.12), and Margaret Solomon interprets III.4, in which the events taking place in the "HCE cube-house" are placed on a film reel, as a form of circling the square.[50]

Another symbol for the alchemical process suggests that it achieves the circling of the square. As previously noted, the alchemists often represented their work as the ouroboros, the serpent biting its own tail, which stands for the circular nature of the work. In a spiritual sense the process forms a circle, with no real beginning or end. As Jung states: "[T]he *opus* . . . is thus in a certain sense a circle like a dragon that bites itself in the tail. For this reason the work is often called *circulare,* or else the *rota,* the wheel."[51] The specific processes of alchemy embody this symbolism, for the major ones consist of circulation in a closed vessel. Of course, there could be no greater mirror of this process than *Finnegans Wake.* As Joyce wrote to Harriet Shaw Weaver on 8 November 1926: "The book really has no beginning or end. . . . It ends in the middle of a sentence and begins in the middle of the same sentence" (*Letters I,* 246). Within this circular book the elements circulate in a literary process of constant vaporizing and condensing, moving from the archetypal to the individual and back again.

Since the alchemists considered the *lapis* a combination of the four elements, its symbol was ⊕ or □⃝. Joyce gave the symbol ⊕ to the ninth question in I.6, a description of *Finnegans Wake.* The symbol □⃝ combines the square, which Joyce assigned to the title of the *Wake,* and the circle, which he assigned to the book of essays *Our Exagmination.* In Margot Norris' view, the two do form a kind of unity, for she sees the critical work as a "veritable extension" of Joyce's book. For her, however, this does not solve the problems of interpretation, but is rather a manifestation of the diverse interpretations Joyce deliberately provided for. In this view, *Our Exagmination* belongs to the *Wake.* As Norris says, Joyce's last book is about the quest for truth and points out the folly of searching for the correct interpretation or the authentic version. The search itself, not its result, is important; therefore the text and this Joyce-supervised book of essays together compose one of the symbols for the *lapis.*[52]

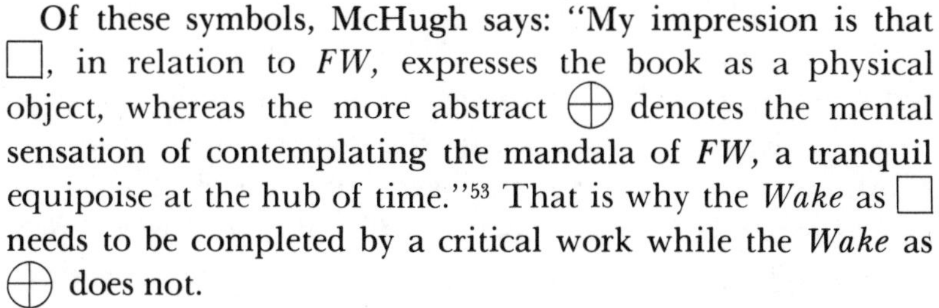

Of these symbols, McHugh says: "My impression is that □, in relation to *FW,* expresses the book as a physical object, whereas the more abstract ⊕ denotes the mental sensation of contemplating the mandala of *FW,* a tranquil equipoise at the hub of time."[53] That is why the *Wake* as □ needs to be completed by a critical work while the *Wake* as ⊕ does not.

Hart also relates the hermitage to which St. Kevin retires (605.04–606.12), Book IV, and *Finnegans Wake* as a whole to the mandala, the symbol ⊕, and therefore the Philosopher's Stone. Speaking of the *Wake*'s "Eternal Now," he says:

> The symbol of the circular universe with its timeless centre is also found in the figure of the Buddhist *mandala* which is of such importance to Jung. This is the symbol ⊕ which, in the MSS, Joyce gave the highly important ninth question in I.6. His use of it to designate a passage dealing with the structure of *Finnegans Wake* suggests that in one structural sense the whole of the book forms a *mandala* . . . in which the four four-part cycles make the Wheel of Fortune, while Book IV lies at the "hub".[54]

The symbol ⊕ denotes not only the mandala, but also the *lapis,* as noted above. The "collideorscape" (143.28) of *Finnegans Wake* resembles a kaleidoscope: "Both, framed in a circle, offer endless rearrangements of a few elements."[55] The enclosing circle is a timeless realm, a state of "suspensive exanimation" (143.08–09) where both alchemical "reconjungation" and "redissolusingness" (143.13,14) take place, where the movement includes both rising and falling. It ends with a rainbow, and specifically with the color violet, which also signifies the achievement of the Stone.

In his comparison of the structure of *Finnegans Wake* to the Eastern and Viconian cycles, Hart unknowingly makes a case for the alchemical cycle as well. According to him, Book I.1–4 is related to earth, Book I.5–8 to water, Book II to fire, and Book III to air; this is also the sequence that the bodies of Eastern adepts supposedly pass through by meditating on AUM, until they reach the final stage of ether. Hart adds, "It will be remembered that this is the ascending order in which Joyce develops the elements in the lesser cycles of *Finnegans Wake,* if Book IV is equated with the ether, which would be quite consistent with its character."[56] The movement through the four elements to ether or the quintessence is precisely that of alchemy. *Splendor Solis* describes the way in which the four elements come together to form the quintessence and adds: "When these five are gathered together, they form ONE substance, whereof is made the natural Stone, while AVICENA contends that: 'if we may get at the fifth, we shall have arrived at the end.'"[57]

Finnegans Wake, then, alchemically brings together four, three, two, and one, forming the Philosopher's Stone by circling the square and solving the ancient insoluble problem of squaring the circle.

Colors and Forgery

The alchemical art began not with the concept of transmutation but of imitation. The 11th *Encyclopedia Britannica* describes its early history:

> In the Leiden museum there are a number of papyri which were found in a tomb at Thebes, written probably in the 3rd century A.D., though their matter is older. Some are in Greek and demotic, and one, of peculiar interest from the chemical point of view, gives a number of receipts, in Greek, for the manipulation of base metals to form alloys which simulate gold and are intended to be used in the manufacture of imitation jewellery. . . . The author of these receipts is not under any delusion that he is transmuting metals; the MS. is merely a workshop manual in which are described processes in daily use for preparing metals for false jewellery, but it argues considerable knowledge of methods of making alloys and colouring metals. It has been suggested by M. P. E. Berthelot that the workers in these processes, which were a monopoly of the priestly caste and were kept strictly secret, though fully aware that their products were not truly gold, were in time led by their success in deceiving the public to deceive themselves also, and to come to believe that they actually had the power of making gold from substances which were not gold. Philosophical sanction and explanation of this belief was then found by bringing it into relation with the theory of the *prima materia,* which was identical in all bodies but received its actual form by

> the adjunction of qualities expressed by the Aristotelian elements—earth, air, fire and water. Some support for this view is gained from study of the alchemistical writings of the period.[1]

By the end of the fourth century, however, writers interpret the processes for coloring metals mystically, and the texts include the idea of transmutation.

Similarly, the notion of the writer as copier or imitator has a long and venerable history. Scribes wrote down the words of others or made additional copies of something already recorded. Of the work in medieval monasteries, Jennifer Schiffer Levine states:

> The manuscripts so long and lovingly worked over were ultimately transcriptions—pious copies of the signature of God. He was the first cause and as such the only significant point of origins for language. Transcription was not theft: it was, rather, a recognition of our dependent and subordinate status.

The modern world promulgated and valued the concept of originality, "yet, as the lines from *Finnegans Wake* [181.14–17] suggest, we may see writing as pious transcription or as deception and theft: total originality, given the shared nature of language, is impossible."[2] Thus, both alchemy and writing involve copying and imitation, and both leave room for charges of forgery and fraud.

The importance of color sequences in alchemy grew out of the theory of the *prima materia* and the attempt to make basic metals resemble gold. Considering black as the absence of qualities, the alchemists sought a black substance at the beginning of the process and manipulated it through a series of color changes to form the Philosopher's Stone; the process moved from black to red or violet. One alchemist states: "In the preparation of Saturn there appears a great variety of different colors; and you must expect to observe successively black, grey, white, yellow, red, and all the different intermediate shades."[3]

Although yellow, the color of gold, would seem the ultimate alchemical aim, a very deep red, violet, purple, or iridescent stage superseded it because it supposedly included all colors. Alchemical writers refer to the *lapis* as a rainbow, and Jung calls it "the diamond whose prism contains all the hues of the rainbow."[4] The Philosopher's Stone regarded as a rainbow also functions within the death-rebirth symbolism of the Hermetic Art. An epigram to an alchemical emblem of the process runs as follows:

> Now the blazing glory of the King gives birth to envy; and a band of ten rustic youths slay him. All things are in confusion, Sun and Moon in darkness reveal many signs of their sadness. There appears the rainbow painted in varied hues, which brings to the people glad tidings of peace.[5]

The emphasis on colors, color sequences, and on the rainbow as both object and symbol parallels Joyce's treatment of color in *Finnegans Wake*. The use of colors in the *Wake* has often been noted by critics, but no one has yet completely accounted for their use either philosophically or concretely. Adaline Glasheen states the problem while at the same time setting forth the most significant uses of color in *Finnegans Wake*:

> I cannot come near to explaining the overall use of the seven colors in *FW*. Sometimes, as I have said, they run alongside the notes of the scale; HCE's number is seven and, as Mr. Kelleher pointed out, HCE always wears seven garments, which must be the seven deadly sins and probably the spectrum itself by way of some Berkeleyan synthesis of subject and object. There are seven Rainbow Girls, distracting and transvestic; a whole section, "The Mime," deals with the colors of good and evil; later (609–13) St. Patrick and Bishop Berkeley . . . speak respectively for the seven colors which fallen man perceives and for the white light which contains all colors. I do not follow Joyce's

> philosophy or his optics, but I assume that saint and philosopher argue Diversity and Unity, Appearance and Reality. Neither wins, but Joyce's interest lies with the many-colored, for History has had little to do with the white radiance of eternity.[6]

No one theory can encompass all of the variety of uses of color in *Finnegans Wake,* but a knowledge of the importance of colors in alchemy sheds a great deal of light on their Joycean use.

The most obvious use of color in *Finnegans Wake* involves the seven Rainbow Girls, "an angel's garland" (226.22–23). They are not only connected with the traditional colors of the rainbow, but also at times the first or last letters of their names or epithets actually spell out the word: "R is Rubretta and A is Arancia, Y is for Yilla and N for greeneriN. B is Boyblue with odalisque O while W waters the fleurettes of novembrance" (226.30–33). Sometimes they reverse direction, and as "Winnie, Olive and Beatrice, Nelly and Ida, Amy and Rue" (227.14) represent the phenomenon of the secondary rainbow, in which the same colors appear, but in the opposite order. Like the alchemists who insisted on the proper succession of colors in their process, Joyce went to great lengths to preserve the proper order of colors in his young female rainbow. The girls the unfortunate Glugg cannot catch are enumerated in the "Mime" chapter: "Not Rose, Sevilla nor Citronelle; not Esmeralde, Pervinca nor Indra; not Viola even nor all of them four themes over" (223.06–08). "Rose" is obviously red; the Seville orange, used for making marmalade, yields "Sevilla" and the color orange; "Citronelle" suggests the fruit and its yellow color; "Esmeralde" contains emerald; "Pervinca" is Italian for "periwinkle," a shrub with a light blue flower; "Indra" suggests indigo; and "Viola" is, of course, violet. Seven Rainbow Girls compose the harem in which ALP's man "spenth his strenth" (also an allusion to HCE's incestuous desires for his daughter): "Poppy Narancy, Giallia,

Chlora, Marinka, Anileen, Parme" (102.25–26). Again Joyce very carefully follows the proper color sequence: the poppy is a red-orange in color, combining the first two hues; "gialla" is "yellow" in Italian; "chloro-" is the combining form for "green"; "Marinka" contains the Spanish and Italian words for "sea," denoting blue; "anil" is indigo, "aniline" a chemical base important in many dyes; "Parme" is the Parma violet, prized for its sweet scent.

A color sequence which ends in violet and forms a metaphorical rainbow stems directly from alchemical theory. The following passage deals with the creation of the *lapis* and also the creation of *Finnegans Wake*:

> Belisha beacon, beckon bright! Usherette, unmesh us! That grene ray of earong it waves us to yonder as the red, blue and yellow flogs time on the domisole, with a blewy blow and a windigo. Where flash becomes word and silents selfloud. (267.12–17)

The alchemical use of colors equates *Finnegans Wake* and the Philosopher's Stone.

Hart notes that Joyce gave the symbol ⊕, also a symbol for the *lapis,* to the answer to question nine in the "Riddles Chapter," a question which deals with the structure of *Finnegans Wake.* That question also ends with a rainbow: "the beau that spun beautiful pales as it palls, what roserude and oragious grows gelb and greem, blue out the ind of it!" (143.24–26). Like the alchemical rainbow, this one also culminates in violet, and, as in alchemy, the color is merely tincture: "Violet's dyed!" (143.26). Violet completes the rainbows of both the *Wake* and of alchemy, rainbows which include all the colors of the spectrum. The alchemical movement from black, or no-color, to white and thence to all colors is expressed in *Bloomefields Blossoms*: "From White into all Colours withouten faile, / Like to the Rainebow or the Peacocks Tayle."[7] *Finnegans Wake,* like the *lapis,* includes everything; its treatment of colors manifests one aspect of this inclusiveness.

Another alchemical use of colors appear at 203.23–29:

> . . . he plunged both of his newly anointed hands, the core of his cushlas, in her singimari saffron strumans of hair, parting them and soothing her and mingling it, that was deepdark and ample like this red bog at sundown. By that Vale Vowclose's lucydlac, the reignbeau's heavenarches arronged orranged her. Afrothdizzying galbs, her enamelled eyes indergoading him on to the vierge violetian.

The entire passage concerns the first time HCE and ALP make love, as well as the first sexual act of the human race. "O happy fault!" (202.34) and "garden of Erin" (203.01) make the Earwickers Adam and Eve, their act of love the fall of all. The sexual imagery is explicitly alchemical, since Humphrey and Anna are also the sun and the moon (202.28–30), the Solar King and Lunar Queen whose sexual union results in the formation of the Stone. Not playing innocent, ALP "indergoads" ("indigo" is her aim) on her "reignbeau," her rainbow, her king, to a violet sexual/alchemical climax.

In Genesis IX:12–17 God establishes the rainbow as the covenant between him and all the living creatures of the earth; in alchemy and in *Finnegans Wake* the rainbow links resurrection, the millennium, and the New Jerusalem. The alchemical rainbow, as we have seen, signifies the rebirth of the king who has been slain and whose appearance "brings to the people glad tidings of peace." The Wakean rainbow also brings about such a revival. For example, on 11.12 it appears in the context of the hen who picks up the pieces after the battle, who puts Humpty Dumpty back together again. "And even if Humpty shell fall frumpty times as awkward again in the beardsboosoloom of all our grand remonstrancers there'll be iggs for the brekkers come to mournhim, sunny side up with care" (12.12–15).

The New Day heralded by St. Patrick's victory over Berkeley also includes a rainbow. Again dawn, eggs, and breakfast testify to a renewal of some sort. Purgation occurs on all levels—"oneguguIp down of the nauseous forere brarkfarsts oboboomaround and you're as paint and spickspan as a rainbow; wreathe the bowl to rid the bowel" (613.22–25). As Tindall notes, the movement here is alchemical: "As above, so below: a bowl of tea will move the bowel."[8] The alchemists began their process with a vile black substance, believing that in it lay the secret of all things; appropriately, then, the rainbow here results from a purging of the bowels. Similarly, Shem makes the ink with which he creates art from his own excrement.

There are other more incidental uses of alchemical colors in *Finnegans Wake.* The appearance of the Rainbow Girls as seven vari-colored gems ("Ruby and beryl and chrysolite, jade, sapphire, jasper and lazul" 494.04–05) has alchemical sanction; in the *Ordinall,* Norton expresses the succession of colors in the alchemical process in terms of crystal, beryl, adamant, magnetia, ruby, amatist, and sapphire.[9] "Xanthos! Xanthos! Xanthos!" (235.09) refers to the *xanthosis* of alchemy, the yellowing process.[10] Since yellow was an intermediate stage in the movement from black to red or violet, the girls in their preference for Chuff/Shaun in this passage and their vision of a future middle-class existence with him indicate their satisfaction with less than a complete transformation.

Another significant thematic link between the alchemical and Wakean use of colors involves fraud. The marriage of the practical work of the Egyptian metallurgists with the Greek philosophy of matter and transmutation produced a hybrid art with myriad possibilities for forgery and deception. Some alchemists dealt overtly with the potentiality for fraud in the coloring process; the overly-defensive Janus Lacinius, in *The New Pearl of Great Price,* gives twenty-six hypothetical objections to alchemy before getting on with his treatise. Number twenty-one is an Aristotelian objection involving color:

> Let me tell the Alchemists that no true change can take place between species; but they can produce things resembling those they desire to imitate; and they can tinge (*i.e.*, colour) with red and orange so as to produce the appearance of gold, and with white so as to produce the appearance of silver (tin or lead). They can also purge away the impurities of lead (so as to make it appear gold or silver); yet it will never be anything but lead; and even though it look like silver, yet its properties will still be those of lead. . . . Moreover, the composition of the various metallic substances is different, and, therefore, it is impossible that one should be changed into another, unless they be first reduced to their common prime substance. But this cannot be brought about by mere liquefaction, though it may appear to be done by the addition of extraneous matter.[11]

Ernst von Meyer articulates the problem well:

> The various colours of the metals, and their alteration by melting them with others, played a prominent part in alchemistic processes; in imparting thereby the colour of a noble metal to a base one, much was supposed to have been attained. For the Alexandrians, therefore, and also for the alchemists of the Middle Ages, the colouring of metals was synonymous with their transmutation. The chief operations were the so-called *Xanthosis, Leukosis* and *Melanosis,* which were compared with the processes followed in the dyeing of cloth. The old designation of tincturae, for the media by which this transformation was brought about, gives expression to the idea that the latter consisted in a dyeing operation.[12]

Since alchemy and writing are inextricably bound in *Finnegans Wake,* the references to alchemical fraud undercut the possibility of complete transformation in the artistic process. If, as we have seen, alchemy springs from a dyeing or tinting process in which metals are merely made to resemble each other, then the whole of alchemy is based on a false premise of the possibility of transmutation. When Joyce employs tinting metaphors or color sequences in reference to writing, he throws the same doubt on the ability of the artist to transform the dross of this life into something transcendent. If Joyce had wanted to present the function of the artist as the perceiver and presenter of truth and transcendent reality he would have used only the Eucharistic metaphor; the mixture of that with the alchemical metaphor shows that he had something more in mind.

The alchemical metaphor undercuts not only blatantly false artists, such as Shaun, who tries to claim his brother's work for his own, but also undercuts Shem, the character who is consistently identified as the artist in *Finnegans Wake.* The only artist who is not undercut is the one who demonstrates an awareness that all art is forgery. Levin states:

> The differences in mood between *Ulysses* and *Finnegans Wake* are underlined by the contrast between the Homeric poems and that prodigious literary hoax, "Makefearsome's Ocean." (294) Joyce's recourse to the Ossianic poems, like his use of the counterfeit word, "hesitancy," evinces a growing addiction to the idea of forgery. Jim the Penman is forging, with a vengeance, the uncreated conscience of his race. His creative ideals have found their unforeseen fulfilment in "an epical forged cheque on the public for his own private profit." (181) The artist, god of his own world, is no better than a criminal in this one, Joyce obliquely admits; the finest literary imitations of life are fakes.[13]

All works of art are fakes in the sense that they are not life; the artist, Norris states, "enjoys no corner on truth; he merely constructs more elaborate and elegant myths and lies more convincingly than the man on the street."[14] Joyce's "elaborate myths" include the lowest and most trivial aspects of life; they manifest the vital relationship between art and life. A work of art, in Joyce's view, should not ignore the everyday, but acknowledge its importance. This is why Stephen is undercut so badly in *Portrait*; his aesthetic theory would make the work of art a self-enclosed static whole with no relation to the artist or the world. In this Joyce differs from Yeats, who in "Rosa Alchemica" states that an understanding that alchemy was actually a philosophy and a spiritual process "enabled me to make my little book a fanciful reverie over the transmutation of life into art, and a cry of measureless desire for a world made wholly of essences."[15]

That Joyce creates a world in his writing also has an alchemical basis. In *An Open Entrance to the Closed Palace of the King* the author describes the alchemical process as parallel to God's creation of the world: "Let the student incline his ear to the united verdict of the Sages, who describe this work as analogous to the Creation of the World."[16] Some critics view Joyce's created world as a transformation of the world of everyday reality; Clive Hart even uses an alchemical metaphor to describe this transmutation in the *Wake*: "Having discovered a formula for the literary philosopher's stone which would allow him to transmute anything into a perfectly integrated element of his novel, he [Joyce] was now able to include the whole universe within the confines of Dublin's hurdles without creating any feeling of strain." Hart also describes Joyce's creation of a glorious new world out of such earthly elements as excrement, sex, and the parts of the anatomy in alchemical terms; for him Joyce creates "a beauty which is distilled by verbal alchemy from obscene scrawls on 'the oozing wall of a urinal'" (*P* 113).[17] But Joyce's use of alchemy in *Finnegans Wake* is more complex; he uses it deliberately as a metaphor for the artistic process to show his understanding that although new worlds may be created, no real transmutation has occurred. This does not mean that art is not possible or valuable, but that Joyce realizes that the basis of art lies in the things of this world, and refuses to forget that or allow his readers to do so.

The close connection of alchemy, writing, and forgery in *Finnegans Wake* is illustrated in the following passage:

> A bone, a pebble, a ramskin; chip them, chap them, cut them up allways; leave them to terracook in the muttheringpot: and Gutenmorg with his cromagnon charter, tintingfast and great primer must once for omniboss step rubrickredd out of the wordpress else is there no virtue more in alcohoran. For that (the rapt one warns) is what papyr is meed of, made of, hides and hints and misses in prints. (20.05–11)

Atherton notes the link of writing and alchemy in the above passage,[18] but his search for another connection for "muttheringpot" beside the alchemical one is unnecessary, because the artist is an alchemist in *Finnegans Wake.* The first printed pages "step rubrickredd out of the wordpress," an allusion to the color sequence of the alchemical process in which red or violet signifies the production of the Stone. "Tintingfast" hints that the work, whether it be that of writing or alchemy, actually consists of nothing more than a dyeing process. The things of this world may be colored, but not transmuted or transcended.

Shem, the artist and alchemist of *Finnegans Wake,* is a forger and a plagiarist. Immediately preceding the section in which he creates his art alchemically this is emphasized: "Who can say how many pseudostylic shamiana, how few or how many of the most venerated public impostures, how very many piously forged palimpsests slipped in the first place by this morbid process from his pelagiarist pen?" (181.36–182.03). Shem then makes ink from his own excrement, searching for the primary black matter which can be impressed with various qualities and thus converted to gold.

In another passage which links writing and forgery the starting point is again excremental. The description of the sleeping Jerry combines his urine and the spilled semen of his wet dream, suggesting he might also use the mixture as ink. "And he has pipettishly bespilled himself from his foundingpen as illspent from inkinghorn" (563.05-06). A few lines later, the word "tintingface" (563.15–16) echoes "tintingfast" (20.08) and connects the whole process to the alchemical with its overtones of dyeing and fraud.

Alchemy, colors, forgery, and plagiarism are united in another passage:

> The diasporation of all pirates and quinconcentrum of a fake like Basilius O'Cormacan MacArty? To camiflag he turned his shirt. Isn't he after borrowing all before him, making friends with everybody red in Rossya, white in Alba and touching every distinguished Ourishman he could ever distinguish before or behind from a Yourishman for the customary halp of a crown and peace? (463.21–27)

"Red" and "white" point to an alchemical interpretation of this passage, for the alchemists often called the opposites which united in the alchemical *vas* the red and white roses. "Basilius O'Cormacan MacArty" is Basilius Valentinus, whose treatise was included in *The Hermetic Museum*. Very possibly Valentinus either was a plagiarist or else never existed. The alchemists constantly borrowed from those who had gone before and attributed tracts to ancient and respected authorities; many alchemical treatises were nothing but amalgamations and plagiarisms of previous ones. Basilius Valentinus may have been one of the arch-alchemical borrowers of all time. Stillman says:

> The question may now be considered as settled beyond reasonable doubt that all the facts and ideas contained in the literature of Basilius Valentinus were compiled after all the works of Paracelsus, Biringuccio, Agricola, Porta, Konrad

> Gesner, and many lesser compilers and writers were in print. From this viewpoint there is little if anything of importance, even in the *Triumphal Chariot of Antimony,* that is not anticipated in these other writers.[19]

More specifically, some modern commentators even doubt the existence of Basilius. A collection of the works of Paracelsus was published in 1589–91; about ten years later a series of treatises appeared under the name of Basilius Valentinus, supposedly a Benedictine monk. The publisher of these tracts, Johann Thölde, claimed he translated the texts from Latin into German and implied that they were early fifteenth century, making them a century earlier than the works of Paracelsus. Since there was a striking similarity between the works of Basilius and Paracelsus, historians assumed that Paracelsus was a plagiarist, and this view was long the accepted one. However, there was no previous mention of Basilius, there was no record of him in the Benedictine register, and Thölde never produced the original manuscript from which he made his translation. After fifty years of research into the subject, H. Kopp, the historian of chemistry, declared the works of Basilius forgeries in 1885; Kopp believes these works are early seventeenth-century forgeries by Thölde.[20]

In this passage Shaun mocks his artistic brother and ridicules Shem's claims of creativity by comparing him to Basilius and accusing him of borrowing all of his ideas from others. Shaun, an opportunist himself, consciously employs an alchemical allusion to undercut his brother, while at other points in this chapter he uses alchemy to inflate himself or achieve his own ends, such as trying to seduce Issy (see p. 77).

The *Wake* contains other important alchemical references which deal with fraud, although not specifically with colors. In this passage one of the four questions the authorship of the letter:

> Or I will let me take it upon myself to suggest to twist the penman's tale posterwise. The gist is the gist of Shaum but the hand is the hand of Sameas. Shan - Shim - Schung. There is a strong suspicion on counterfeit Kevin and we all remember ye in childhood's reverye. 'Tis the bells of scandal that gave tune to grumble over him and someone between me and thee. He would preach to the two turkies and dipdip all the dindians, this master the abbey, and give gold tidings to all that are in the bonze age of anteproresurrectionism to entrust their easter neappearance to Borsaiolini's house of hatcraft. He is our sent on the firm. Now, have you reasonable hesitancy in your mind about him after fourpriest redmass or are you in your post? Tell me andat sans dismay. (483.01–14)

This passage identifies Shaun as the false alchemist who tries to claim the work of Shem as his own and who takes advantage of the people by preaching a false doctrine. Alchemy and writing are again connected, as they are so often in *Finnegans Wake* (20.05–10, 182.30–186.18). Not only is Shaun, the "counterfeit Kevin," allied with the forger Piggott ("hesitancy"), but he is also identified with a false alchemist. In *The Ordinall of Alchimy* Thomas Norton relates the tale of a monk who claimed to possess the secret of the Hermetic Art and claimed that within forty days he would erect fifteen abbeys on Salisbury Plain to prove it. However,

> When forty dayes were gone and past,
> The *Monkes* Crafte was cleane overcast.
> Then all his *Abbies* and all his thought,
> Was turned to a thing of nought;
> And as he came, he went full lewde,
> Departing in a mind full shrewd:
> For soone after within a little while,
> Many trewe men he did beguile;
> And afterwards went into *Fraunce*.[21]

Shaun here acts as "master the abbey," spreading the "gold tidings" of alchemy, but his art proves as false as that of Norton's monk.

The reception of the king in III.4 contains a number of alchemical allusions. Among them are "aureal" (568.20), "By the splendour of Sole!" (568.29), "his miniated vellum" (568.31–32), "that illuminatured one" (568.33–34), and "Senior Nowno and Senior Brolano" (569.32), references to *Splendor Solis,* a sixteenth-century vellum illuminated manuscript with allegorical pictures of the alchemical process now in the British Museum. Its twentieth-century editor, intent on proving its authenticity and value, refers to it as "Trismosin's Alchemical Process called the Red Lion, and given at length in the AUREUM VELLUS, published Rohrschach, 1598, also in the TOISON D'OR, 1602 and 1622, as summarized by Professor Schneider in his History of Alchemy, 1832, and veiled in the pictures and treatises of SPLENDOR SOLIS. . . ."[22] The *OED* defines "miniate" as "to color or paint with vermilion; to rubricate or (in extended sense) to illuminate (a manuscript)." Joyce plays on both meanings. "When I came to the end of the work I found such a beautiful red colour as no scarlet can compare with," Trismosin says;[23] and, as already noted, *Splendor Solis* was an illuminated manuscript. The alchemical text often quotes the alchemist Senior, here amalgamated with Browne and Nolan, the Dublin bookseller. Again the shadow of forgery looms over the entire passage, for some historians of chemistry consider this work spurious, believe that the reputed author, Trismosin, never existed, and that all tracts published under his name are impostures. J. K., the modern annotator of *Splendor Solis,* seems acutely aware of the text's susceptibility to such attacks. Quite defensively, he states his belief that the work was executed under the direction of Trismosin, or, if not, could have been done by an artist encouraged by an amateur alchemist. Then, afraid he may have undercut his own argument, he adds the afterthought that perhaps all of the writings attributed to Trismosin *except* the *Splendor Solis* and the tale of his wanderings which precede it are spurious or have been tampered with. Next, he uses Trismosin's account of his wanderings in search of the Philosopher's Stone as proof of the text's authenticity, arguing that his travels account for the Venetian palaces and Italian landscapes in the allegorical illustrations. Finally, he caps his argument with internal evidence: "If he was not an Adept and only a fraud, why the Manuscript with its calm sensible writing, not intended for publication? Why the artistic paintings of undoubted merit?"[24] The air of falsity in the *Wake* is increased by the fact that the king, to whom HCE reads from the manuscript, takes the alchemical instructions literally as the puffers do; there follows a very real attempt at sexual union ("joking up with his tonguespitz to the crimosing balkonladies, here's a help undo their modest stays with a fullbelow may the funnyfeelbelong" 569.01–03).

The dialogue between Archdruid Berkeley and St. Patrick is one of the most difficult passages in *Finnegans Wake*. The rising sun illuminates a stained-glass triptych of the meeting of Berkeley and Patrick and the legends of St. Kevin and St. Lawrence O'Toole. Joyce told Budgen that the one window represented "the meeting of St Patrick (Japanese) and the (Chinese) Archdruid Bulkely (this by the way is all about colour)."[25] Critics have interpreted the outcome and meaning of the argument differently, however. Edward A. Kopper asserts "the importance of reading the ending of *FW* as the triumph to Patrick's reason over the Druids' mysticism." Séan Golden, who notes that both the *Tunc* page and the *Quoniam* page of the Book of Kells appear in the passage (611.04, 10), feels that the discussion, "which centers on the rainbow and colors, is also a discussion of Irish illuminated art." James Atherton states:

> The concept in the passage "topside joss pidgin fella Balkelly" (611.04) that the colour of an object is no part of its real nature,

or alternatively is its only reality, may also derive from alchemical thought although its context suggests the works of Berkeley and some possible oriental source as well.[26]

The alchemical reference elucidates the Berkeley-Patrick debate, helping to explain the nature and outcome of the discussion as well as to illustrate the significance of the passage in terms of Joyce's view of art and the artist. In fact, in the dialogue Joyce seems to have been following a specific alchemical text, *The New Chemical Light* of Michael Sendivogius, a treatise included in *The Hermetic Museum.*

Since interpretations of this passage vary so widely, it will be helpful to review it before proceeding with the alchemical allusions. "Balkelly, archdruid of islish chinchinjoss" (611.05) represents the philosopher Berkeley, whose main tenet was "*esse est percipi,*" as well as the druids defeated by Patrick in his Christianizing of Ireland. The seer, according to the Archdruid, sees the "true inwardness of reality" (611.21); he perceives all seven colors, the six colors which have been absorbed by an object as well as the color which it has been unable to absorb and thus can be perceived by ordinary human perception. Attired "in the his heptachromatic sevenhued septicoloured roranyellgreenlindigan mantle" (611.05–07), which indicates his position as a "seer," he perceives the essence of things rather than their appearance. To St. Patrick, however, who perceives only the outward reality, the seer's clothes are all green: "the his essixcoloured holmgrewnworsteds costume the his fellow saffron pettikilt look same hue of boiled spinasses" (611.35–36). Still, St. Patrick's shortsightedness might unknowingly partake in an inner reality as well. In Tindall's interpretation, "whatever an Irishman wears outside, inside he is wearing the green."[27] Also, in one of the contests between St. Patrick and the druids, J. B. Bury detects a memory of the fertility cults in which a victim, who represented the spirit of vegetation, was sacrificed that the crops might be fruitful.[28] Thus, the archdruid King Leary, representative of the pagan cults in the struggle against Christianity, has a green essence in spite of his outer appearance; in the confrontation he becomes the pagan god of fertility.

In his reply Patrick derides the Archdruid as a "Bigseer" (612.16) who is "aposterioprismically apatstrophied and paralogically periparolysed" (612.19–20); he is atrophied and paralyzed by his arguing from effects to causes and by his false reasoning. This leads the Archdruid both to assume an object's existence because it can be perceived by our senses, and to assume what cannot be proven—for example, that while we can perceive only one color, the inner reality is that there are six more. Patrick in an extremely complicated passage ironically still manages to cut through the philosophical obfuscation about the seven colors to arrive at a simple, practical solution. The primary manifestation of the seven colors, the rainbow, is the sensible symbol of the fire of the sun, says Patrick. We perceive the rainbow when the sun shines through drops of water vapor. In this case, we do not see only one color and have to perceive the others in the mind's eye; rather, we physically see the entire spectrum. Therefore we *know* that sunlight is composed of seven colors. Patrick worships the rainbow as "Balenoarch . . . Great Balenoarch . . . Greatest Great Balenoarch" (612.27–28), reversing the Italian word for rainbow, "arcobaleno," to combine it with the idea of Noah's Ark and the flood. The practicality of St. Patrick manifests itself again in his use of the shamrock to teach the doctrine of the Trinity.

The alchemical doctrine of colors underlies this debate, as Atherton has noted. Sometimes the alchemists regarded color as an accidental quality, not an essential one. This is the archdruidical view—that the color of an object does not express its real nature, which only the seer can divine. The alchemists believed that everything was potentially gold; they tried physically to show forth this essence when they attempted to transmute base metals into gold. They were, then, in Berkeley's sense, "seers." On the other hand, the fact that the alchemists continually attempted to tinge or tint their materials to have them resemble gold indicates that in a practical sense they considered color to be of the real nature of a thing; a metal could not be gold unless it resembled gold.

The Berkeley-Patrick dialogue can be interpreted through an alchemical work which deals with these problems, *The New Chemical Light Drawn from the Fountain of Nature and of Manual Experience* by Michael Sendivogious, which Joyce seems to be following rather closely. The treatise speaks of a "seed" by which objects multiply themselves: "Now, the nature of this seed which is produced out of the four elements, is threefold: it is either *Mineral,* or *Vegetable,* or *Animal.*"[29] Berkeley explains to Patrick the illusions of the furniture of the world in its mineral, vegetable, and animal aspects; interestingly, Joyce originally wrote "animal, vegetable, and mineral," but later reversed the order to accord with the alchemical text.[30] Sendivogius continues his alchemical tract by explaining the nature of the seed which all metals contain and which presumably can bring the metals to their full potential, gold. In this discussion he distinguishes between the vulgar, who do not believe what they cannot see, and those, like himself, who can perceive inner reality:

> Nature brings forth Mineral or Metallic seed in the bowels of the earth. This is the reason why so many will not believe in its existence—because it is invisible. And on this account the vulgar unbelief is not so greatly to be wondered at: for if they hardly understand that which is openly before their eyes, how should they know anything about that which they cannot see. Yet, whether they believe it or not, the fact remains the same, and it is most true that that which is above is as that which is

below, and that which is born above has origin from the same source which is at work down below, even in the bowels of the earth.[31]

The relationship of this to the Archdruid Berkeley's point of view is obvious.

The seed contained by all metals is mercury, yet it is not common mercury, and the author of *The New Chemical Light* uses this distinction to separate those with common perception from the seers. He states: "Thus metals are indeed generated out of mercury; but those ignorant persons who say that this first substance of metals is ordinary mercury, confound the whole body with the seed that is in it, seeing that common mercury, too, contains metallic seed, as well as the other metals."[32]

At the end of the "Tenth Treatise" Sendivogius says: "Now let us advance from theory to practice," informing the reader that the "Eleventh Treatise" concerns "the practical preparation of our Stone or Tincture by means of our Art."[33] The movement parallels that of the Berkeley-Patrick debate in the *Wake,* when the arguments of the practical saint follow those of the mystical archdruid. In fact, the course of the argument follows *The New Chemical Light* even in the seven colors giving way to green. During the alchemical process, the worker should: "Regulate the heat judiciously, until there appear colours like those of the Peacock's Tail; and then continue to apply this well-regulated heat until the colours resolve themselves into a pronounced green."[34]

Lest the literal-minded reader think that this really is a practical treatise, *The New Chemical Light* continues with an emphasis on inward reality and the metaphor of seeing so important in the Berkeley-Patrick dialogue:

Consider, I pray you, the simple water of the clouds. Who would believe that it contains in itself all mundane objects,

> hard stones, salts, air, earth, and fire? What shall I say of the earth, which seems simple enough, and yet contains water, fire, salts, air, and much besides? O, admirable Nature, who knowest by the means of water how to produce the wonderful fruits of earth, who dost give life to them and nourish them by means of air! Everything depends upon the faculty of seeing which we bring to the study of Nature. Common eyes, for instance, discern that the sun is hot; the eyes of the Sage see that the sun itself is cold, and that it is only in its movements which produce heat; for its effect is felt at so great a distance in space.[35]

This dialogue was one of the first sections of *Finnegans Wake* composed by Joyce; however, although he wrote it in 1923, he did not use it in the manuscript until 1938 (*Letters I*, 202n). Joyce himself asserted the importance of this section in a letter to Harriet Weaver: "I work as much as I can because these are not fragments but active elements and when they are more and a little older they will begin to fuse of themselves" (*Letters I*, 205). Thus, the alchemical allusions were part of the generating elements of *Finnegans Wake* from the very beginning, and it is not surprising to find all of the alchemical references added to pages 182–86 in a typescript dated February 1924 (see pp. 9–10).

Later Joyce emphasized the significance of this passage in a letter to Frank Budgen:

> Much more is intended in the colloquy between Berkeley the arch druid and his pidgin speech and Patrick the arch priest and his Nippon English. It is also the defence and indictment of the book itself, B's theory of colours and Patrick's practical solution of the problem. Hence the phrase in the preceding Mutt and Jeff banter "Dies is Dorminus master"=Deus est Dominus noster plus the day is Lord over sleep, i.e. when it days. (*Letters I*, 406)

Tindall believes that Berkeley is the artist/Shem and Patrick the practical man/Shaun. If so, then the artist defends the book while the public attacks it.[36] The identification of the artist with the alchemist is consistent with the alchemical metaphor in *Finnegans Wake*; both concern themselves with transmutation. But this is precisely why the public, and Joyce himself, condemn such works. The fact that the artist figure, Berkeley, alludes to *The New Chemical Light* bears out this interpretation, for this alchemical text is of the spiritual and allegorical sort which largely composes *The Hermetic Museum*. Transmutation of metals into gold is not the aim of this work; that physical event, should it occur, merely acts as the prelude to "profounder and more advanced study."[37] Such mystical alchemical texts represent to Joyce a false type of art. As Joyce points out, in reference to the Muta-Juva dialogue, "the day is Lord over sleep"—the everyday elements of life cannot be ignored. At this point in the book the daylight triumphs, heralding a new day which combines the "trancefixureashone" and the "Feist of Tabornecceles" (613.09). The readings on the Feast of Tabernacles include passages about the dawn of a new day and the life-giving water of Zion. When the Lord comes to fight the enemies of Jerusalem:

> . . . it shall come to pass in that day, *that* the light shall not be clear, *nor* dark:
>
> But it shall be one day which shall be known to the LORD, not day, nor night: but it shall come to pass, *that* at evening time it shall be light.
>
> And it shall be in that day, *that* living waters shall go out from Jerusalem. (Zech. 14:6–8)

The judgment against those who do not worship the Lord is that they shall have no rain (Zech. 14:17). The other readings on this day, Ezekiel 47 and John 37ff. also concern the life-giving water of Zion. Together, the light of the Transfiguration and the water of the Feast of Tabernacles form the rainbow (613.24), symbol of the new day.

Patrick triumphs over Berkeley, but his practical solution will not stand long. The day will not always triumph over night, the practical person over the artist/alchemist. The awakening is more of a reorganization than a regeneration: "Yet is no body present here which was not there before. Only is order othered. Nought is nulled. *Fuitfiat!*" (613.13–14). *Finnegans Wake* ends with the dawn, but immediately flows back to the beginning of the cycle. Still, this functions as a necessary antidote to the theoretical, abstract view of reality propounded by the alchemist Berkeley. It indicates Joyce's belief that any art which claims to express only inner essence or which aims at total transcendence to the complete exclusion of the here-and-now must fail; he uses the alchemical allusions to present his case.[38]

Colors function in *Finnegans Wake* to identify the *Wake* with the *lapis,* the result of the alchemical process; Joyce's use of the rainbow and the "New Jerusalem" theme in connection with it makes this clear. But while equating the book with the alchemical goal, Joyce also presents a view of the artist which includes a great many references to forgery and fraud. Alchemical theories and uses of color cannot be separated from charges of tingeing and dyeing, and throw doubt on the possibility of transmutation. When Joyce identifies the artist and the alchemist he also throws doubt on the ability of the artist to transmute the dross of this earth into alchemical gold. Art can create a new world out of the things of this one but should not forget its source or substitute the created world for the real one.

Ingredients and Equipment

Alchemical ingredients appear with surprising frequency in *Finnegans Wake*. Joyce follows the dual alchemical tradition, using references both to vile substances and to chemical ones. In some cases ingredients function on a surface level, enriching the texture of the book, while in other cases they work on a much deeper level, thematically, structurally, and stylistically. Joyce utilizes them as the alchemists did, for both literal and symbolic purposes; in fact, the mixture of things from which Joyce composes his book—songs, nursery rhymes, ads, radio programs, different languages, geometry problems, and geography, for example—parallels the odd mixtures of the alchemists.

In some cases references to substances used by the alchemists function only as atmosphere in *Finnegans Wake*. Most of the alchemical ingredients which permeate the pages concerning Shem the "alshemist" are of this type, for example "Brimstone Walk" (182.31), "calicohydrants of zolfor" (182.36–183.01), "lees of whine" (183.32–33), "globules of mercury" (183.35), and "mercery" (184.09). Alchemists used lees of wine in the production of verdigris (see p. 110); Shem's lees are of "whine" because he is a coward who to avoid fighting "kuskykorked himself up tight in his inkbattle house, badly the worse for boosegas" (176.30–31). "Brimstone" is sulphur; "zolfor" contains "zolfo," Italian for sulphur. Mercury and sulphur, both common and philosophic, had an important place in practically all alchemical experiments; they constituted the physical and spiritual opposites necessary to the formation of the Stone. Mercury, however, also assumed a great significance in and of itself; it was the *prima materia,* the goal, the process in between.[1] Appropriately, all of these ingredients appear in this section as the things out of which Shem creates his art.

Shem possesses an alchemical personality; the text describes him as having a "costive Satan's antimonian manganese limolitmious nature" (184.36–185.01). A metallic element used in alchemical operations, antimony, like most alchemical ingredients, was considered both a physical element and a spiritual set of properties. Manganese is a grayish-white metallic element, whose oxide gives toughness to steel in the alloying process, but Joyce could also be alluding to "magnetia," which Norton claimed was an essential ingredient of the Stone (see p. 131). "Limo" is a combining form meaning "clayey" (*OED*); alchemists who regarded the process as spiritual called the dark part of the mind from which the purified soul would rise the *limus profundi.* Chemists employ litmus, obtained from lichens, in certain chemical tests, for in alkaline solutions it remains blue, while in acid solutions it turns red. Also, Shem's nature alchemically includes opposing elements, for instance both constipation ("costive") and the means of relieving it ("manganese" suggests "magnesia")—hence Shem's "wildgoup's chase across the kathartic ocean" (185.06).

The references to alchemical ingredients function on a thematic level by strengthening and expanding the basic patterns and motifs of *Finnegans Wake.* Specifically, allusions to alchemical substances used for tinting metals bring to bear all the possibilities for fraud inherent in alchemy and in the artistic process analogous to it and also function as accusations, taunts, and proofs of guilt against the various characters in *Finnegans Wake*. In a passage describing the body of the recumbent giant Finnegan in terms of the landscape, his feet are "swarded in verdigrass." He is a hero and yet a fake; he has "clay feet" (7.30); his blood which is sacramentally drunk is "fraudstuff" (7.13) and merely a "goodridhirring" (7.19). The allusion to verdigris emphasizes this theme. Verdigris is a green or greenish-blue substance used as a pigment, in dyeing, and in medicine, significant to the alchemists because of their belief in the importance of color and color changes in metallic transmutations. To make verdigris the alchemists placed copper over the lees of wine and then scraped off the resulting rust.[2] Thus, the color change resulted from the formation of rust on the copper rather than from transmutation. This reference, then, works with the others in the passage, undermining Finn's credibility as a hero and model.

Later Shaun is accused of crimes involving painting and tingeing. As with the other allusions to alchemical ingredients involving coloring, his defense, with an allusion to "verdigrease" (412.33), only compounds his guilt. The early metallurgists used verdigris to color stones to make them resemble precious gems; however, the stains resulting from these operations were often not permanent, so the workers then subjected the stones to mordanting solutions to fix the color. The earliest manuscripts describing these procedures became the basis for alchemy and later for the belief in transmutation and the theory that color changes proved transmutation. The early alchemist Zosimus, who appears several times in *Finnegans Wake*, mentions verdigris, as does the Canon's Yeoman, and Basil Valentine may have inspired Joyce's spelling of the word (he writes "verdigreece").[3]

The reference to verdigris occurs in Shaun's answer to two questions that accuse him of being a dyer. First the people state that he has "painted our town a wearing greenridinghued" (411.24), then that both the furniture and verdure of the town have been varnished (412.10–12). In reply, Shaun claims he will reorganize the post office to make it run more efficiently. Under the previous postmaster, the goats continually ate the "quipu," an ancient Peruvian device to record events or keep accounts which consists of a cord with knotted strings of different colors; therefore, Shaun, like the alchemists, seeks a way to fix dyes more permanently. He admits, though, that his powers are not great enough to solve the problem completely. Confronted with the dyeing charge, he responds:

> —It is a confoundyous injective so to say, Shaun the fiery boy shouted, naturally incensed, as he shook the red pepper out of his auricles. And another time please confine your glaring intinuations to some other mordant body. What on the physiog of this furnaced planet would I be doing besides your verjuice? That is more than I can fix, for the teom bihan, anyway. (412.13–18)

Perhaps Shaun reacts so violently to questions that seem more or less innocuous because of the aura of fraud which surrounds the processes of dyeing and tinting, especially in regard to their relationship to alchemy.

HCE condemns instead of defends himself in I.4 by the mention of copperas and alum. Accused of disguising himself and impersonating others, he explains how "all the sulfeit of copperas had fallen off him quatz unaccountably like the chrystalisations of Alum on Even while he was trying for to stick fire to himcell" (86.02–05). Both copperas and alum are used in dyes; the alchemists purified them in the process of perfecting metals into gold. HCE's statement associates him with the dyeing proces of alchemy; no wonder his alchemical disguise falls off.

Alchemical references pervade this entire passage. At the trial, HCE or Festy King appears "soaked in methylated . . . appatently ambrosi*aurealised*" (85.31–32, my emphasis). For his defense, he takes on the guise of the sixteenth-century alchemist and physician Philippus *Aureolus* Paracelsus. The first to apply the word "alcohol" to what we now know as alcoholic beverages, Paracelsus indulged freely in them. He spent much of his life wandering, "lodging at public inns, drinking to excess, but still performing admirable cures. Oporinus testifies that even during the period of his professorship he never seemed sober."[4]

Both Paracelsus and the defendant at this trial readily assume new names and identities. The name "Philippus Aureolus Paracelsus" was self-bestowed. "Paracelsus" means "greater than Celsus"—the sixteenth-century physician wanted to distinguish his medicine, based on experiment and experience, from that of the first-century physician Celsus and those who relied solely on such ancient authorities for their medical theory and practice. Also, Paracelsus "exhausted his ingenuity in transpositions of letters and abbreviations of words and sentences. For example, when he wrote *subtratur* he meant tartar, and *mutrin* meant nitrum, and so on."[5] Taking a cue from the alchemist, the defendant at the trial in the *Wake* forms his "illassumed names of Tykingfest and Rabworc" (86.12–13) by scrambling and reversing his name, Festy King, and his alias, Crowbar.

The testimony of various witnesses brings in a reference to "basel" (88.05), site of Paracelsus' trial. A professor of medicine at the university there, Paracelsus was tried and expelled because he challenged the blind reliance on ancient medical authorities and advocated observation and experiment instead. In the *Wake*'s trial, the prosecutor questions the validity of the defendant's B.A. degree, as the authorities in Basel questioned Paracelsus' medical degree. The alchemist and physician remained a persecuted man his entire life: the other doctors forced him to leave Strasburg for curing a man who was thought incurable, the medical faculty at Nuremburg prohibited the sale of his book *The French Malady,* the priests forced him to flee from Switzerland, and the authorities refused him permission to practice medicine in Innsbruck.[6] This suggests the way in which his accusers continually hound, accuse, discuss, and insult HCE in *Finnegans Wake.*

Shaun alludes to alum later in the book to cut down his brother; his long invective against Shem includes the "alum that winters on his top" (423.23–24)—he accuses Shem of having dyed hair and/or a wig. The reference to alchemy once again concerns dyeing and supplements the strong forgery theme in the book.

In II.i, the girls flirt with Glugg, but reveal their real intentions through the reference to "hematite" (247.35–36), which appears in a list of twenty-eight taunts they throw at him. Hematite, iron oxide, is red in its powdered state. Iron oxide reds are used generally as pigments; thus, hematite is one of the jeers of the "prettimaid tints" (247.34). The girls mock and tempt Glugg—they lure him with their colors, but ultimately desire Chuff. Two other references to iron oxide concern HCE and his various manifestations; as "oxhide or Iren" (127.26) it is one of the clues to the first riddle, the answer to which is "Finn MacCool," and as "oxsight of Iren" (392.27) it is connected to "Matt Emeritus," who has the hermaphroditic characteristics of HCE. The dye causes HCE to appear under these different guises, as in alchemy dyes made other metals resemble gold.

"Cinnabar" ("zinnzabar" 182.09), another alchemical ingredient important because of its color, functions in several ways and on several thematic levels in *Finnegans Wake.*

Formed by the combination of mercury and sulphur, cinnabar or mercuric sulphide is a brilliant red; because of its color it had great significance for the Graeco-Egyptian alchemists, since they considered the achievement of red the end of the alchemical process. After many attempts these two elements, symbolizing the opposing forces of fire and water, might be joined: "And at last the alchemist, by aid of the kerotakis of Mary and the mysterious sublimation process, did succeed in causing the union of sublimed sulphur with mercury in the kerotakis cup; and the product was a color more brilliant than any heretofore obtained, the red or scarlet of artificial sulphide of mercury."[7] It appears, significantly, in a passage in which Shaun excoriates his artistic brother Shem, accusing him of being a forger and a plagiarist, and directly before the passage in which Shem is called an "alshemist" (185.35). Cinnabar, then, functions as an alchemical element, as a manifestation of the coloring and dyeing theme of both alchemy and the *Wake,* and as an emblem of the union of opposites.

The reference to arsenic and bismuth ("this prime white arsenic with bissemate alloyed" 577.04), another union of opposites, is explicitly sexual, and functions in the immediate context to foreshadow the physical union of HCE and ALP and in the larger context to indicate that both male and female are necessary components of any whole. The alchemists worked with both arsenic and bismuth in their experiments; MacArthur explains the nature of the alchemical conjunction:

> White arsenic is arsenious oxide, highly poisonous (but can be taken in controlled doses as a medicine . . .); bismite is bismuth oxide (bismuth compounds are also used medicinally). Arsenic, often an ambivalent symbol, originally meant masculine, strong, and together with prime is thus associated with the male. 'Bissemate' suggests a twofold feminine nature (cf. 242.16 'biss', 284.23, etc.) supported by the traditional association of woman with the number two. The passage can thus be seen as a

> union of poison and curative, male and female, one and two, whose essential unity is reinforced because arsenic and bismuth are chemically very similar elements.[8]

As HCE and ALP go downstairs to bed, then, their approaching union is described in the alchemical terms of arsenic and bismuth: they are the elements combined in the alchemical retort; they are the King and Queen whose union brings about the consummation of the Great Work.

On one occasion, during one of the many speeches in which HCE defends himself against all the various accusations made against him, he uses the sexual metaphor of alchemy as a justification for his actions. In his apologia for himself and his life, HCE describes love as a tennis game, framing it in the alchemical terms of the union of gold and silver ("my goldrush gainst her silvernetss" 366.11). By their association with the sun and the moon, gold and silver became the opposites whose marriage formed the Philosopher's Stone.[9] HCE follows his allusion to these two metals by an admission of his incestuous desires for his daughter (366.13–15), also an alchemical justification since the alchemical process was often represented as being incestuous. The self-defense of HCE in this section thus includes references to the alchemical tradition, where sexual activity similar to that of which he is accused attempts to achieve a transcendent union of opposites. These references, however, incriminate rather than acquit HCE, for alchemy is deeply imbedded in the network of forgery and sexual activity in *Finnegans Wake*. That the alchemical sexual union may have been metaphorical or used for a higher purpose does not negate the guilt of HCE; rather, it emphasizes the universality of such guilt. The cycle of fall and rebirth and the concept of the *felix culpa* are essential to alchemy and to *Finnegans Wake*.

The references to salts in the *Wake* also reflect the thematic use of alchemy, specifically the reconciliation of opposites. Ian MacArthur states:

> Salts in general are formed from the reactions of acids and bases (alkalis), opposites in modern chemistry and similarly regarded by mediaeval 'puffers' (183.12) (alchemists). Joyce uses this idea a number of times:
> (i) 59.17 'Achburn, Soulpetre and Ashreborn' forming a triad (two opposites and their combination);
> (ii) 167.19 saltpetre is formed from nitric acid and potash (an alkali);
> (iii) 185.33 'gallic acid on iron ore' forms a salt present in ink (iron oxide being a base). This may also combine a reference to language since gallic can mean Gaelic or French and iron is often associated with Erin, e.g. at 547.32;
> (iv) 393.01 'acid and alkolic; signs on the salt, . . .'.[10]

Shem's ink, as MacArthur notes above, contains one of these salts (185.33); therefore, the artist in *Finnegans Wake* writes with an alchemical combination of opposites.

At times such alchemical references serve a number of thematic purposes, for example "Messrs Achburn, Soulpetre and Ashreborn" (59.17–18). Not only do contrary elements go into the formation of saltpeter, but Joyce's particular expression of this triad associates it with the phoenix and hence the death and rebirth motif important in alchemy and in the *Wake*. "Burn" and "ashreborn" suggest the alchemical process symbolized by the phoenix, the destruction of the body of a substance by fire and its rebirth as spirit and gold. Saltpeter literally means "salt of the rock," but Joyce transforms it into "soul of the rock," referring to the alchemical belief that the labors of the alchemist released the soul of the metal from its gross physical body, and bringing in the physical and spiritual aspects of alchemy which function throughout the *Wake*.

References to "Glauber's salt" or sodium sulphate deal with the problem of unity in diversity as well; the reference at 168.08 concerns the question of whether the brothers are distinct or are one and the same (see p. 74). "Acid and alkolic; signs on the salt" (393.01–02) alludes to the same treatise.[11] This reference appears in the "Matt Emeritus" section of "Mamalujo," which contains many such combinations of opposites: "Poor Matt" is a "perigrime matriarch, and a queenly man" (392.19–20); saltpeter ("soldpowder" 393.22) is used for destruction (in gunpowder) and growth and health (as a fertilizer and a diaphoretic medicine); and "alum and oves" (393.24) combines alum, a chemical ingredient used by alchemists, with eggs, a "vile" ingredient used by the "puffers." Fittingly, all these occur in a chapter in which the four garrulous and senile old men each give a version of the coupling of Tristan and Iseult, which they lasciviously observe. Both the alchemical allusions and the Wakean exploration of this mythic love story deal with the relationship between unity and diversity.

According to some alchemists, mercury, sulphur, and salt composed all things; therefore, they were necessary ingredients in the alchemical process. These three major alchemical elements occur in the passage "swifter as mercury he wheels right round starnly . . . Till first he sighed (and how ill soufered!) and they nearly cried (the salt of the earth!)" (454.20–25). Mercury, sulphur, and salt are here expressed in terms of movement, sighs, and tears, representing the literal and everyday aspect of the Great Work. Also, they occur in the "in-between" stage of Jaun's sermon—after the main body, but before the "postlude," suggesting the transcendent nature of the union of these three elements.[12] Paracelsus related them to the view that body, spirit, and soul constituted all matter; salt he equated to the body, mercury to the spirit, and sulphur to the soul. "Corrosive sublimate" ("corrosive sublimation"

185.36) is mercuric chloride, a suitable form of sophic salt to be combined with sophic sulphur and mercury to perform the alchemical work.[13] Thus, it was one of the three elements which the alchemists combined to form a unity.

"Lithargogalenu" (184.13) stands for two things that are actually one, again emphasizing the theme of unity in diversity, but also contains stylistic implications for the *Wake*. The alchemists often used litharge in their work; Norton thought it a necessary ingredient for the preparation of the Stone, and the Canon's Yeoman mentions it as one of the ingredients he and his master use (1. 775, p. 216). Galena (lead sulphide) was used in the preparation of silver. Together, litharge and galena represent two things which are yet one, making their combination by Joyce and their use in *Finnegans Wake* appropriate. Stillman notes:

> Lead, plumbum nigrum, its occurrence in connection with silver, its uses in making certain bronzes, for making lead water pipes, and in sheet form, are described by Pliny. Its oxide (Pb O) is described under the names of molybdaena, lithargyros, and galena, as the product of roasting lead in the air, and as produced in the furnaces where silver and gold are smelted.[14]

Galena also seemed to give empirical proof of the theory of transmutation:

> . . . the mineral galena (lead sulphide) possesses the colour and lustre of lead, but it is neither malleable nor fusible like lead. When it is heated, however, it disengages sulphureous fumes, acquires the missing properties, and is transformed into lead. Could not lead by further heating, or further treatment, be made to lose more sulphur and be endowed thereby with other properties which would ennoble it further to silver, and eventually to gold? As it happens, lead from galena often contains considerable quantities of silver, which may be separated from it by further heating in the process of cupellation. Such observations, suggesting an actual conversion of part

of the lead into silver, confirmed the faith of the transmutationists.[15]

Similarly, in Joyce's art, words contain or suggest other words and the traits of different characters overlap, suggesting transmutation. For example, "Fiendish park" (196.11) reveals Phoenix Park as the site of a sinister sexual sin, while HCE, buried in a "watery grave" (78.19), becomes Lycidas, Alonso in *The Tempest,* the drowned man in *Ulysses,* and other victims of drowning. As in the silver which results from the heating of lead described above, however, no real transmutation has taken place. The words, characters, and situations remain themselves while suggesting manifold other possibilities.

The reference to "alum and oves" (393.24) previously discussed in the context of the reconciliation of opposites also exemplifies Joyce's use of alchemical ingredients in stylistic and structural ways. The combination of a real chemical element with a common substance reflects the dual nature of alchemy, its physical and spiritual aspects. This entire chapter of *Finnegans Wake* concerns sexual union, and the Tristan-Iseult story which underlies it has both its physical and spiritual aspects, as did the sexual union which symbolized the alchemical process. A. E. Waite claims that some alchemists could not complete the Great Work because they could not find the "elect woman who was necessary thereto," and Flamel supposedly only achieved the *magnum opus* with the help of his wife Parnella. Campbell describes the nature of the relationship: ". . . the work of the alchemist was intimately personal, and where it involved the cooperation of an actual woman in the mythic role of *regina, soror, filia mystica,* the relationship was necessarily, because of its psychological dimension, deeply personal and exclusive."[16] Possibly the human alchemical couple metaphorically or physically acted out the union of opposites which took place in the alchemical vessel.

Joyce reflects his awareness of the relationship between the alchemical work, the sex act, and fall and rebirth by his frequent and conscious confusion of alum and Adam, and its coupling with Eve. Besides this reference at 393.24, this idea also appears at 86.04 and 377.16. By equating the sin of Adam and Eve, the story of Tristan and Iseult, the alchemical process, and the story of HCE and his family, Joyce shows the universality of his themes and the consubstantiality of the human experience. He accomplishes this stylistically, by confusing "alum" and "Adam," by having this occur on one occasion in the chapter dealing with Tristan and Iseult, and by hinting throughout the book by confusion of names, references, and similar characteristics that any and all sexual sins are the sins of HCE. That is why the nature of his sin in the Park is never clearly delineated.

A reference to mercury also points to the stylistic and structural implications of alchemy in *Finnegans Wake.* One of Issy's footnotes in the "Lessons Chapter" reads: "Mater Mary Mercerycordial of the Dripping Nipples, milk's a queer arrangement" (260.F2). This note, with its allusion to the alchemical element of mercury, indicates that the road of history, expressed in the text in terms of great men, is also the circular road of alchemy. Like *Finnegans Wake* and the Viconian road, alchemy ends where it begins, and mercury stands as the primary symbol of this concept. In addition, Issy's footnote comically affirms the need for the nurturing female, left out of the dry, scholarly procession of history in the text; similarly, the female is essential, both metaphorically and literally, in the alchemical process.

Issy asserts the need for the female to complete the alchemical process in another footnote as well. She writes, "Tho' I have one just like that to home, deadleaf brown with quicksilver appliques, would whollymost applissiate a nice shiny sleekysilk out of that slippering snake charmeuse" (271.F5). "Deadleaf brown" refers to litharge, "a subtill Earth, browne, roddy, and not bright."[17] The alchemists often symbolized quicksilver or mercury as a snake, serpent, or dragon, both in their writings and their illustrations, often as the dragon that devours itself, or as two dragons consuming each other.[18] In her footnote Issy discloses that she desires not just quicksilver applique on her dress, but one completely made of snakeskin. She wants not just a surface transformation, but a real one. Clothed in the serpent skin, she can help reveal the secrets of alchemy and transmutation. This footnote to a passage concerning the Garden of Eden reminds us that male and female were both necessary parts of the alchemical process, just as they are essential aspects of the human condition portrayed in the *Wake*.

Some alchemical materials are concrete and particular and yet embody the entire alchemical process at the same time. Mercury (183.35, 184.09), already discussed, and vitriol ("blueygreyned vitroil's" 603.35) exemplify this type of substance. Like many alchemical terms, vitriol refers to the spiritual and physical properties shared by a number of substances as well as to one substance in particular. Basilius Valentinus and other writers expressed the nature of this substance in the "vitriol acrostic":

> The fullest form of this was as follows, but the last two words were often omitted: *Visitabis interiora terrae, rectificando invenies occultum lapidem, veram medicinam.* The initials thus gave the word *Vitriolum.* . . . "Visit the inward parts of the earth; by rectifying thou shalt find the hidden Stone, the true Medicine": some of the adepts held that this formula concealed the whole secret of the Great Work and its material; but they differed greatly among themselves in their interpretation of the word "vitriol", which was a generic term applied to a large variety of substances.[19]

Vitriol is thus a fitting element to show forth the legend of St. Kevin on the stained-glass window, for he, like each character in *Finnegans Wake,* is "someone imparticular who will somewherise for the whole" (602.07).

These alchemical allusions to mercury and vitriol, therefore, parallel Joyce's use of words, a technique in which a word is individual and unique and yet emblematic of the entire work. The vigil at which Tim Finnegan is waked is also where he wakes. In fact, the word "wake" encompasses the total action and meaning of *Finnegans Wake*; that is why Joyce placed such importance on the title of the book and guarded it jealously for so long. By equating "alum" with "Adam," Joyce suggests the alchemical belief in the fallen nature of metals and their resurrection as gold, the fall of Adam and Eve, the Incarnation, and the death and resurrection of Christ. "Alum" thus implies Christian, mythic, and alchemical death and rebirth, all of which operate microcosmically and macrocosmically in *Finnegans Wake.*

One final allusion to alchemical ingredients is "Sugars of lead for the chloras ashpots!" (616.12). MacArthur has tentatively identified these chemicals as sugar of lead (lead acetate) and potassium chloride.[20] Since some of the uses of sugar of lead are "with alum as a mordant in dyeing and printing cottons . . . manufacturing varnishes . . . manufacture of chrome pigments; ingredient of hair dyes,"[21] the alchemists may have used it in their search for a tincturing agent. An early alchemical text does describe the production and use of sugar of lead:

> Zosimus . . . describes quite intelligibly the preparation of white lead from litharge and vinegar; the first product of this reaction, sugar of lead or lead acetate, is correctly said to be both sweet and salt-like, and, on keeping, to change slowly into white lead.[22]

Potassium chloride is a source for potassium salts, but seems to have no alchemical uses. This passage, the final form the letter takes in *Finnegans Wake,* concerns chemical rather than alchemical combinations. A man who is made a "carpus of" cannot be put completely back together, "in contravention to the constancy of chemical combinations" (616.06, 07–08), but since he has been a child HCE has possessed "highest valency" (616.13), the greatest degree of combining power possible. Fittingly, alchemy gives way to chemistry in this ricorso chapter, for the cycle will continue, just as alchemy united "the dialytically separated elements of precedent decomposition for the verypetpurpose of subsequent recombination" (614.33–35).

Alchemical equipment appears infrequently, but always meaningfully, in *Finnegans Wake.* Shem cooks the ingredients of his art in an athanor (184.18), a type of alchemical furnace. The alchemists used many different furnaces, each necessary for a certain process or to obtain a specific degree of heat; in the athanor the vessel containing the matter to be heated was placed in a pan full of ashes. The alchemical vessel in which the most important part of the process took place was called a *vas*; fittingly, Shem uses a *vas* to make his ink (185.19). The sublimation process took place in the aludel (299.L1).

The alchemists also called the vessel in which the alchemical ingredients were mixed and cooked a "retort." An allusion to this occurs in the "Lessons Chapter": "As I was saying, while retorting thanks, you make me a reborn of the cards" (304.26–28). Kev has just struck and knocked down his brother Dolph. Instead of attempting revenge, Dolph forgives his brother; since a fall must come before resurrection, he credits Kev with aiding in his rebirth, doing so in alchemical terms. Shaun/Kev's marginal notation also suggests that the fight has brought reconciliation instead of further opposition: "*The rotary processus and its reestablishment of reciprocities.*" This expresses the ongoing cyclical nature of life, *Finnegans Wake,* and alchemy.

The "*altare cum balneo*" (605.08) of St. Kevin also has an alchemical basis; some alchemists called the vessel in which the union of opposites took place the "King's Bath."[23] In this passage, St. Kevin sits meditating in a bath. Campbell and Robinson state: "The act of the saint is a cherubical combination of baptism, the Mass, and marriage."[24] It is also an alchemical act; once again the alchemical and priestly roles intermingle as they do when Shem transforms his own excrement into ink and then into art. In the alchemical illustration on the next page, the King and Queen sit in a bath, representing the purification and commingling essential to the work.[25] St. Kevin eschews the need for a queen; the marriage which takes place in the alchemical bath will be for him a "celibate matrimony" (605.09), but the use of the marriage theme points out that his actions are alchemical as well as religious. In his bath St. Kevin meditates upon the religious and alchemical rebirth which will result: "he meditated continuously with seraphic ardour the primal sacrament of baptism or the regeneration of all man by affusion of water" (606.10–12). He sits there "when violet vesper vailed" (606.04), violet being the color which symbolized the consummation of the alchemical process.

Allusions to alchemical ingredients and equipment function on a number of levels in *Finnegans Wake.* They are used thematically, to strengthen and emphasize the prominent themes of the book such as fraud and the reconciliation of opposites. They suggest a circular structure whose end is its beginning, and vice versa, and they also provide Joyce with a stylistic paradigm embodying the relationship of constituents to the whole and the particular and the universal.

Illustration 3. The King and Queen in the Bath, representing the union of opposites of the alchemical process. Note the symbols for the Sun and Moon, associated with the King and Queen, respectively, in the upper corners. From the *Viridarium Chymicum* by Michaelis Meyeri (Frankfurt, 1688), p. 103. Reprinted by permission of the British Library, London.

Shem the "Alshemist"

The densest concentration of alchemical allusions in *Finnegans Wake* occurs on pages 182–86. This is fitting, because it is in this section that Shem the "alshemist" makes ink from his own excrement. Father Robert Boyle has explicated page 185 in terms of the Eucharistic metaphor,[1] but there is another level of metaphor in this passage, and that is the alchemical; the Eucharistic union of infinite and finite is produced by alchemical means. In this passage Joyce explicitly equates the artistic and alchemical processes, and indicates that any view of art or the artist derived from *Finnegans Wake* must take cognizance of the use he makes of the Hermetic Art. The passage also contains most of the alchemical themes utilized in the *Wake,* including the use of colors, the use of excrement, and the themes of forgery and fraud. Therefore, in contrast to the rest of this study, this section cuts across thematic divisions to consider these pages as a unit, dealing with the various aspects of alchemy as they occur. An alchemical explication of these pages will show how Joyce uses alchemy both as a reference pattern and as a metaphor for the artistic process in *Finnegans Wake.*

Shem the "alshemist" (185.35) is an "evilsmeller" who creates "rancid Shem stuff" (182.17); his house is "a stinksome inkenstink, quite puzzonal to the wrottel" (183.06–07). Ripley says of some alchemists: "Men may them smell for multyplyers where they go."[2] The Canon's Yeoman tells a similar tale concerning his master:

> And everemoore, where that evere they goon,
> Men may hem knowe by smel of brymstoon.
> For al the world they stynken as a goot;
> Hir savour is so rammyssh and so hoot
> That though a man from hem a mile be,
> The savour wole infecte hym, trusteth me.
> (11. 884–89, p. 217)

"Puzzo" is the Italian word for "stink," and besides sulphur, alchemists used other materials which could have added to the smell which issued from their workshops and from them. They used dung for fuel, they used human waste in their mixtures, and they used organic animal and vegetable matter for various procedures, including putrefaction and fermentation.

References to alchemists and alchemical terms, processes, materials, and equipment permeate this section. Shem, "devoted to Uldfadar Sardanapalus" (182.18), pays homage to the Assyrian King whose library provided an important repository for the chemical texts which became the basis for alchemical theory.[3] His house is on "Brimstone Walk" (182.31); in the "Canon's Yeoman's Tale," we learn that "Arsenyk, sal armonyak, and brymstoon" (1. 798, p. 216) are among the ingredients used by alchemists. Brimstone, another term for sulphur, was a basic alchemical ingredient. Also, Shem's address, "Asia in Ireland" (182.31), is fitting for an alchemist, for although the evidence is strong that the idea of transmutation began with the Alexandrian Greeks, "the alchemy which embraced it as a leading principle was also strongly affected by Eastern influences such as magic and astrology. The earliest Greek alchemistical writings abound with references to Oriental authorities and traditions."[4]

"The soulcontracted son of the secret cell" (182.34–35) describes an alchemist who jealously guards the secret of his art and perches precariously on the brink of heresy. Alchemical historians cite the stories of numerous alchemists who "groped through life at the expense of the taxpayers" (182.35), as Shem did. Alchemists often gained the favor of kings and emperors, who gave them tremendous amounts of money from state treasuries to carry out their experiments, often supporting them for years in the hope that they would transmute base metals into gold and thus free the country from economic worry. The "calicohydrants of zolfor and scoppialamina by full and forty Queasisanos" (182.36–183.02) with which Shem works have alchemical overtones as well. Calcination was a major alchemical process in which a solid was reduced to a powder by the application of heat. Sulphur was a basic alchemical ingredient, and "scoppialamina" suggests the Italian "scoppiare in lagrime," to burst into tears, probably the alchemist's reaction to an unsuccessful transmutation.[5] Alchemical texts stress the importance of the number forty in the Hermetic Art. The seventeenth-century treatise *The Sophic Hydrolith,* which gives directions for making the Philosopher's Stone, directs the worker to combine the ingredients and then leave them for forty days; this treatise also discusses the general magical significance of this number.[6]

Alchemical references dot the long list of things which litter Shem's house and go into his art. The fact that his house is "persianly literatured" gives a clue to his method; under Alexander the Great, the Greeks conquered Persia, as well as the rest of the ancient world, and then founded Alexandria, which was the way in which alchemy eventually came to be transmitted to the West. Holmyard states:

> The transmission was made chiefly through direct contact in Alexandria and other Egyptian cities, but partly by intercourse

> with the intellectual centres of Harran, Nisibin, and Edessa in western Mesopotamia. This subsidiary channel helps to explain the unmistakable traces of Persian and even Assyrian influence in Muslim alchemy, manifested by linguistic affinities in technical terms and usages and in names of minerals. . . .[7]

Also, the fact that Shem fills the "warped flooring of the lair and soundconducting walls thereof, to say nothing of the uprights and imposts" (183.08–10) with the elements of his literature recalls Zosimus' report on the knowledge and practice of alchemy in Alexandrian Egypt. As Holmyard explains it:

> He tells us that the chemical arts were practised in Egypt under royal and priestly control, and that it was illegal to publish any work on the subject. Only Bolos Democritos had dared to infringe this regulation; as for the priests themselves, they had incised their secrets on the walls of the temples and pyramids in hieroglyphic characters, so that even if any seekers after forbidden knowledge were venturesome enough to brave the darkness of the sanctuaries they would have found the inscriptions unintelligible.[8]

"Puffers" (183.12) are listed among the components of Shem's writing, and Holmyard says: "It was a common obsession with the alchemists that if they could but get a sufficiently high temperature, transmutation would be easy. They therefore used bellows to such an extent as to earn the nickname of *souffleurs*, 'puffers', bestowed upon them by the cynical."[9] The word "soufflosion," which appears at 184.30, strengthens this association. "Imeffible tries at speech unasyllabled" (183.14–15) is a literary equivalent of the Philosopher's Stone, while "solid objects cast at goblins" (183.21–22) brings to mind the more magical side of alchemy and the fact that alchemists were accustomed to having visions. Alchemists, as well as Shem, used "tress clippings" (183.29) in their art; "cans of Swiss condensed bilk" (183.30) recall the idea of forgery and fraud as it relates both to the alchemists and to Joyce's conception of the artist; and "deoxodised carbons" (183.33) and "globules of mercury" (183.35) are undistorted alchemical elements.

The fact that Shem is "self exiled in upon his ego" (184.06–07) hints that the artist's process of writing about himself is an alchemical one. This suggests the spiritual and psychological side of alchemy, in which the aim is the perfection of the human soul, or, according to C. G. Jung, the creation of a new "self" by the process of individuation. During this procedure Shem undergoes "a nightlong a shaking betwixtween white or reddr hawrors, noondayterrorised to skin and bone by an ineluctable phantom" (184.07–09). White and red were two important stages in the preparation of the Stone; sometimes alchemists regarded these two colors as the opposites which went into the formation of the *lapis*. Norton says of the process: "Then is the faire White Woman / Married to the Ruddy Man."[10] Similarly, Ripley asks the reader to: "Consyder fyrst the Latytude of thy Precyous *Stone, / . . . .* Where the *Red Man* and the *Whyte Woman* be made one."[11]

This section may also contain an allusion to the *Book of Mercy,* a treatise written by a disciple of the Arabian alchemist Gheber or Djäber, although the author credits the book to Djäber himself. It begins: "'The Book of Mercy by Abou Musa Djäber ben Hayyan El Dumaouï El Azdi Eç Confi. May God be merciful to him.'"[12] A denunciation of those who neglect their souls to amass gold and silver follows. "In the same work, however, there are vague allusions to the red elixir and the white elixir, terms conventionally used by alchemists to indicate preparations supposed to convert base metal into gold and silver."[13] Thus, Shem stands "betwixtween white and reddr hawrors" and it is asked that "the Shaper have mercery on him" (184.07, 09).

Joyce also alludes directly to *The Ordinall of Alchimy* by Thomas Norton ("Anglican ordinal" 185.10), for the alchemist states that "litharge" ("lithargogalenu" 184.13) and "magnetia" ("manganese" 184.36) are the two essential ingredients needed to prepare the *lapis*. Litharge, as noted before, is "a subtill Earth, browne, roddy, and not bright," while magnetia is "a Stone glittering with perspecuitie, / Being of wonderfull Diaphanitie."[14]

The "white or reddr hawrors" (184.07–08) between which Shem the alchemist stands are, then, the White and Red Elixirs which transmute base metals into silver or gold or the elixirs which give immortal life (they had both properties). In a like manner, Shem tries with his alchemy to transmute a strange and varied conglomeration of ingredients into literary gold, and he thus attempts to make himself immortal as well.

The process by which Shem produces his art is explained in detail several times. We learn that he,

> . . . by the dodginess of his lentern, brooled and cocked and potched in an athanor, whites and yolks and yilks and whotes to the frulling fredonnance of *Mas blanca que la blanca hermana* and *Amarilla, muy bien,* with cinnamon and locusts and wild beeswax and liquorice and Carrageen moss and blaster of Barry's and Asther's mess and Huster's micture and Yellownan's embrocation and Pinkingtone's patty and stardust and sinner's tears, acuredent to Sharadan's *Art of Panning,* chanting, for all regale to the like of the legs he left behind with Litty fun Letty fan Leven, his cantraps of fermented words, abracadabra calubra culorum . . . (184.17–26).

So, with reliance on Dodgson and on Sheridan's *Art of Punning* Shem produces his literature, again using both his own peculiar literary style and the alchemical process. An "athanor," in which he does his cooking, is an alchemical furnace, described in detail in *An Open Entrance to the Closed Palace of the King,* and, appropriately for Shem's art,

Bloomefields Blossoms calls the athanor the "*Philosophers Dunghill.*"[15] The Spanish words which he mutters as a kind of spell refer to the colors of the different stages in the production of the Philosopher's Stone. "Whiter than the white sister," he says, and then, "Yellow, very good," both of which preceded the last stage of red or purple. Beeswax was used in alchemical writing in Greece, making its appearance here very appropriate,[16] and "fermentation," as previously noted, was an important alchemical process. By intoning "abracadabra," Shem invokes the

> magic triangle of pagan Theosophists . . . to which they attributed extraordinary virtues and represented as follows:
>
> ABRACADABRA
ABRACADABR
ABRACADAB
ABRACADA
ABRACAD
ABRACA
ABRAC
ABRA
ABR
AB
A.[17]

Like the literal-minded alchemists, Shem seeks his art in excrement and urine ("Asther's mess and Huster's micture"), as well as in myriad types of eggs. He prepares his "oves and uves à la Sulphate de Soude" (184.29), that is, with sodium sulphate, or Glauber's salt.[18] Johann Rudolph Glauber (1604–68) furthered chemistry by his practical observations and experiments, but also believed in the possibility of transmutation and the existence of an elixir which could convert any metal into gold. He claimed that his salt was this alkahest or universal solvent. No wonder Shem prepares his eggs with Glauber's salt. Antimony ("antimonian" 184.36) was important to the alchemists. In *The Triumphal Chariot of Antimony,* Basil Valentine claims great power for this element; not only can it make one rich by the achievement of the Philosopher's Stone, but it is also the "true medicine," which soothes wounds and ulcers, cures impure blood, "makes glad the heart, excites chastity and honesty," and cures the "French disease," leprosy, melancholy, and madness.[19]

"Messrs Codex and Podex" (185.03) are fitting legal advisors, for "codex," which in general is a manuscript volume, is the word attached to many alchemical texts, and "podex" means "anus" or "rectum" in Latin, foreshadowing the process by which Shem makes his ink a few lines later. "Father Flammeus Falconer" (185.04), besides being the Dublin printer who, as Glasheen notes, burned the sheets of *Dubliners,* may be the fourteenth-century alchemist Nicholas Flamel. Flamel would be an agreeable character to Joyce, for many people believed that he and his wife Parnella had gained immortality through his discovery of the elixir. In "Rosa Alchemica," Yeats talks of "Flamel, who with his wife Parnella achieved the elixir many hundreds of years ago, and is fabled to live still in Arabia among the Dervishes."[20] Both Parnella and the Irish hero whom his countrymen refused to leave in the grave ("Some say he is not in that grave at all. That the coffin was filled with stones. That one day he will come again." *U* 112) may be referred to in the "prattlepate parnella" who "kills time" (173.11). Outwardly, the passage attacks the artist/alshemist who also attempts to "kill time" with his art.

Father Boyle is undoubtedly correct in ascribing the Latin passage in which Shem makes ink out of his own waste to the Church's penchant for disguising "in the language of blushfed porporates" (185.09–10) anything which might corrupt the minds of her children. Another source for this passage, however, might be the need of the alchemists to write obscurely to prevent the unworthy from using this powerful knowledge wrongly. Also, many alchemists state that their knowledge is ineffable and can only be expressed obliquely. The author of the sixteenth-century *Rosarium Philosophorum* says: "So I have not declared all that appears and is necessary in this work, because there are things of which a man may not speak. . . . Such matters must be transmitted in mystical terms, like employing fables and parables."[21]

The "Anglican ordinal" (185.10), as mentioned before, refers to Thomas Norton's *The Ordinall of Alchimy,* which was included in Ashmole's *Theatrum Chemicum Britannicum* in 1652 and was reprinted by A. E. Waite in *The Hermetic Museum* in 1893. Norton makes a point of saying that he is writing so that only the educated, not the ordinary person, will understand. In the "Proheme" he implores the reader not to change a word of his writing, while emphasizing the rightness of each syllable:

> For where quick sentence shall seame not to be
> Ther may wise men finde selcouthe previtye;
> And chaunging of some one sillable
> May make this Boke unprofitable.[22]

Joyce would have been pleased to discover that the *Ordinall* was not signed, and that the author's name is found by combining the first letters of the chapters.

The use of excrement in the Latin passage again allies Shem's process to alchemy, when Shem makes his ink and thus his entire world from his own waste. Similarly, "the alchemists sought their *prima materia* in excrement, one of the arcane substances from which it was hoped that the mystic figure of the *filius philosophorum* would emerge."[23] Referring to alchemy, Jung says of truth, goodness, and beauty that: "They are not always found where we look for them:

often they are hidden in the dirt or are in the keeping of the dragon. 'In stercore invenitur' (it is found in filth) runs an alchemical dictum—nor is it any the less valuable on that account."[24] Of course, the alchemists did not use their own wastes as Shem does; the making of this "alshemist's" ink emphasizes his solipsism. Joyce makes the point that Shem is a sham artist/alchemist.

The close association between excrement and the loftiest goal, the Philosopher's Stone, is explained by psychoanalysis in terms of sublimation (185.36); the pun on the alchemical process of sublimation is obvious and delightful. (See pp. 54–59 for a description of sublimation and Joyce's use of it as a literary technique.) In explaining the psychoanalytic concept of sublimation Norman O. Brown talks of "Freud's theorem on the identity of what is highest and lowest in human nature. In Freud's language: 'Thus it is that what belongs to the lowest depths in the minds of each one of us is changed, through this formation of the ideal, into what we value highest in the human soul.'" Or, to put it another way, "the basic structure of sublimation is, to use the psychoanalytical formula, displacement from below upward."[25] Therefore, the basic Hermetic dictum, "As above, so below, as below, so above," is confined largely to the latter movement in the world of psychoanalysis, although Joyce hermetically allows the double movement.

Concerning the phrase "*in vas olim honorabile tristitiae posuit*" (185.19–20), Father Boyle says, "In the second draft, Joyce wrote: 'in poculum vasum olim honoribilem tristitiae posuit.' His first notion was, apparently, 'poculum tristitiae,' 'cup of sadness.' 'Poculum' he changed to 'vasum' probably because this word can mean a container in a sexual context—even more so in the form 'vas.'"[26] The alchemical container, as previously mentioned, is also referred to as a "*vas*" and is often compared to a womb. Campbell says:

The mystic vessel, *vas Hermeticum,* represented in the various retorts within which the transmutations came to pass, was regarded with the utmost religious awe as a virginal womb, fertilized by the spirit Mercurius, a veritable *vas mirabile,* and likened to (or even called) the Tree of the Fruit of Immortal Life, and in some of the later, fifteenth- and sixteenth-century texts, the Cross of Christ, or Mary's womb.[27]

Then we are told how Shem "transaccidentates" himself and thus is present in substance in his writing. That an alchemical process has been used to obtain this Eucharistic end is fitting, for as early as the end of the fifteenth century alchemy and the Mass were seen as related. The entire third section of Jung's *Psychology and Alchemy* concerns the parallels between Christ and the alchemical *lapis.* Many alchemists were very explicit about this identification; a large part of *The Sophic Hydrolith* expounds the analogy between the Stone and Christ, stating, "We shall thus understand that the earthly philosophical stone is the true image of the real, spiritual, and heavenly stone Jesus Christ."[28]

Shem, "the first till last alshemist" (185.34–35) seems to successfully accomplish an alchemical end—from his own individual person and life he creates all of history and an all-embracing universal eternal work of art. However, "the squidself which he had squirtscreened from the crystalline world waned chagreenold and doriangrayer in its dudhud" (186.06–08). The reference to Dorian Gray undercuts his artistic accomplishment, and the magic words used to effect the transformation become mere gibberish ("And dabal take dabnal! And the dal dabal dab aldanabal!" 186.09–10). Shem makes one last attempt at the alchemical pasttime of "circling the square" (186.12) and is compared to the third-century Alexandrian alchemist Zosimus ("if what is sauce for the zassy is souse for the zazimas" 186.16), but, as Shaun has reminded us, "Shem was a sham and a low sham" (170.25–26); and, as

Joyce has reminded us, the ingredients of Shem's art include "puffers" (183.12). Shem is a sham/Shem artist and alchemist.

In fact, all artists and alchemists who work to transcend and transmute and therefore escape the world by means of their art are shams. The artist/alchemist, however, can unite the physical and the spiritual by operating on both levels simultaneously, turning the rubbish of life into art or the Philosopher's Stone, yet not ignoring or negating its earthly origins. As *Finnegans Wake* puts it: "The tasks above are as the flasks below, saith the emerald canticle of Hermes . . ." (263.21–22).

Notes

Introduction

1. H. Stanley Redgrove, *Alchemy: Ancient and Modern,* 2nd ed. (London: William Rider & Son, 1922), p. 1.

2. Hugh Munro Ross, "Alchemy," *Encyclopedia Britannica,* 11th edition (1910–11).

3. *The Golden Tract Concerning the Stone of the Philosophers,* in *The Hermetic Museum,* ed. Arthur Edward Waite, 2 vols. (London: James Elliott, 1893), I, 19; hereafter cited as *HM.*

4. *Prelude to Chemistry,* 2nd ed. (London, 1936; rpt. Cambridge, Mass.: MIT Press, 1961), p. 135.

5. Thomas Norton, *The Ordinall of Alchimy,* in *Theatrum Chemicum Britannicum,* ed. Elias Ashmole, The Sources of Science, No. 39 (1652; rpt. London: Johnson Reprint Corporation, 1962), p. 39; hereafter cited as *TCB.*

6. Solomon Trismosin, *Splendor Solis* (London: Kegan Paul, Trench, Trubner & Co., [1920]), p. 88.

7. James S. Atherton, *The Books at the Wake* (N.Y.: Viking Press, 1960), p. 47.

8. Thomas E. Connolly, *The Personal Library of James Joyce,* University of Buffalo Studies, 22 (1955), 5–58; Richard Ellmann, *The Consciousness of James Joyce* (London: Faber & Faber, 1977), pp. 97–134.

9. Preface, *HM,* I, ix.

10. *James Joyce's "Ulysses"* (N.Y.: Vintage Books, 1955), p. vii.

11. "James Joyce and the Hermetic Tradition," *A Journal of the*

History of Ideas, 15 (1954), 28; *Transcendental Magic,* trans., annotated, intro. A. E. Waite (1896; rpt. London: Rider & Co., 1968), p. 1.

12. Hélène Cixous, *The Exile of James Joyce,* trans. Sally A. J. Purcell (N.Y.: David Lewis, 1972), p. 647.

13. *Alchemy,* p. 1.

14. Introduction, *Scribbledehobble* (Evanston, Ill.: Northwestern University Press, 1961), pp. xvi–xvii.

15. David Hayman dates these drafts in *A First-Draft Version of "Finnegans Wake"* (Austin: University of Texas Press, 1963), p. 300.

16. Material in brackets is added in pencil in Joyce's hand on left-hand page facing typescript.

17. For Joyce's method of composition, see Connolly, Introduction, *Scribbledehobble,* pp. vii–xxii.

18. For example, Mark Troy relates all of these to Egyptian themes in *Mummeries of Resurrection* (Uppsala: University of Uppsala, 1976).

The Excremental Vision: Spiritual and Physical Alchemy

1. *The New Pearl of Great Price,* the original Aldine ed. trans. into English (London: James Elliott, 1894), pp. 111–12.

2. *The Alchemical Writings,* ed., trans. A. E. Waite (Hamburg, 1676; rpt. London: James Elliott, 1893), p. 95.

3. As with most aspects of *Finnegans Wake,* the rubbish heap has other realistic and mythical predecessors; my concern here, however, is only with the alchemical allusion. For several other sources for the dung-heap, see John Garvin, *James Joyce's Disunited Kingdom and the Irish Dimension* (Dublin: Gill & Macmillan, 1976), pp. 121–22, 204.

4. W. Y. Tindall, *A Reader's Guide to "Finnegans Wake"* (N.Y.: Farrar, Straus, and Giroux, 1969), p. 44.

5. Tindall, *Reader's Guide,* p. 39.

6. *Reader's Guide,* p. 45.

7. *The Integration of the Personality,* trans. Stanley Dell (London: Lowe & Brydone, 1940), p. 268.

8. Walter L. Wilmhurst, Introduction (1918), M. A. Atwood, *Hermetic Philosophy and Alchemy,* re-issue of *The Suggestive*

Inquiry Into the Hermetic Mystery (1850; rpt. N.Y.: Julian Press, 1960), p. 26.

9. *Early Poems and Stories* (London: Macmillan, 1925), pp. 465–66.

10. *The Only True Way,* in *HM,* I, 151–52.

11. *Golden Tract,* in *HM,* I, 20.

12. *The Only True Way,* in *HM,* I, 152.

13. C. G. Jung, *The Psychology of the Transference,* trans. R. F. C. Hull (Princeton: Princeton University Press, 1954), p. 5.

14. *Psychology and Alchemy,* Vol. XII of *The Collected Works of C. G. Jung,* trans. R. F. C. Hull, 2nd ed., Bollingen Series XX (Princeton: Princeton University Press, 1970), p. 182.

15. *Psychology and Alchemy,* p. 245.

16. *Psychology and Alchemy,* pp. 19, 18.

17. *Psychology and Alchemy,* pp. 258, 270–72.

18. *Psychology and Alchemy,* p. 250.

19. C. G. Jung, "Transformation Symbolism in the Mass," in *Psyche and Symbol,* trans. R. F. C. Hull and Monica Curtis, ed. Violet S. de Laszlo (Garden City, N.Y.: Doubleday, 1958), p. 195.

20. Richard Ellmann, *James Joyce* (N.Y.: Oxford University Press, 1959), p. 557. .

21. *The Decentered Universe of "Finnegans Wake"* (Baltimore: Johns Hopkins University Press, 1974), p. 91.

22. Ruth Von Phul, "Mummer in Motley," lecture given at State University of New York at Binghamton, 25 April 1972.

23. Ellmann, *James Joyce,* pp. 480–83.

24. *Structure and Motif in "Finnegans Wake"* (London: Faber & Faber, 1962), pp. 25–26. For other views of *Finnegans Wake* as confession, see Matthew Hodgart, *James Joyce* (London: Routledge & Kegan Paul, 1978), p. 134; Cixous, p. 23. A related view of the way in which the artist shares himself is found in Robert Boyle, *James Joyce's Pauline Vision* (Carbondale: Southern Ill. University Press, 1978), p. 43: "More than Pater, more even than Wilde and Hopkins, Joyce sees the end of literature as being the dynamic sharing of the heights and depths of the necessarily lonely unique Word—i.e., the self."

25. *Psychology and Alchemy,* p. 23.

26. *Psychology and Alchemy,* p. 23.

27. *Integration of the Personality,* p. 259.

28. "Esthetics of Dedalus and Bloom: Nineteenth Century Roots,

Structural Metaphors, and Resolutions," Diss. SUNY Binghamton 1974, pp. 9–10. Other critics have expressed similar interpretations of Joyce's view of art. Robert Boyle, "The Artist as Balzacian Ass," in *A Conceptual Guide to "Finnegans Wake,"* ed. Michael H. Begnal and Fritz Senn (University Park: Penn. State University Press, 1974), p. 76, analyzes the Shem chapter by illuminating the references to Balzac and Wilde; he points out that Joyce accepts rather than rejects human experience, with its elements of good and evil. Cixous gives Stephen much more credit than I do for being a true artist (see esp. p. 355), but she also sees Joyce as resolving the mind/body dualism in his works (p. 635). Ellmann, *The Consciousness of James Joyce,* pp. 75–76, 83, notes that Joyce rejects any "partial art," "displaying the collusion between the brutal materialism of Buck Mulligan, his indifference to the consequences of his acts and words, and the mysticism of George Russell, for whom acts done in this world are merely lying semblances," although he too reads the end of *Portrait* differently than I do and thinks more of Stephen. Darcy O'Brien, *The Conscience of James Joyce* (Princeton: Princeton University Press, 1968), pp. 23, 27, 49, states that Joyce criticizes Stephen's attempt to escape the sordid aspects of life, but could not himself reconcile love and lust, the physical and the spiritual.

"As Above, So Below," and Death and Rebirth

1. Francis Llewellyn Griffith, "Thoth," *Encyclopedia Britannica,* 11th edition, XXVI, 882. Frances Boldereff, *Hermes to His Son Thoth* (Woodward, Pa.: Classic Non-Fiction Library, 1968), performs a strange and rather mystical explication of Joyce's use of Thoth and Giordano Bruno. Bruno, Boldereff states, believed passionately in the Hermetic doctrine, and claims that Hermes, in fact, wrote the *Shadows of Ideas.* Rightly, then, Joyce identified himself with Thoth, to whom the *Corpus Hermeticum* refers as the son of Hermes (pp. 30–31). Boldereff lists many references to Bruno's thought in *Finnegans Wake,* and explicates the geometric diagram on page 293 in Brunonian terms. The book posits an ongoing philosophical and mystical tradition exemplified by Egyptian religion, Bruno's writings, Joyce's works, and Klee's paintings.

2. Tindall, "James Joyce and the Hermetic Tradition," p. 23.

3. Ross, "Alchemy," 11th *Encyclopedia Britannica,* I, 519.
4. Redgrove, *Alchemy,* pp. 40–41.
5. In Cixous' appendix, "Thoth and the Written Word," pp. 737–45, she uses the story of Thoth to discuss the relationship between Shem and Shaun. She also deals with Thoth's association with writing and from it derives Joyce's attitude to the written word. For a list of references to Hermes and Thoth in *Finnegans Wake,* see Boldereff, pp. 31–33; Adaline Glasheen, *Third Census of "Finnegans Wake"* (Berkeley: University of California Press, 1977), pp. 126, 282; Troy, pp. 56–57; Arthur T. Broes, "More People at the Wake (Contd.)," *A Wake Newslitter,* 4 (1967), p. 29.
6. Glasheen, *Third Census,* p. 282.
7. Joseph Campbell and Henry Morton Robinson, *A Skeleton Key to "Finnegans Wake"* (N.Y.: Viking Press, 1944), p. 62n.
8. Glasheen, *Third Census,* p. xxxii.
9. Read, p. 135.
10. *The Compound of Alchymie,* in *TCB,* pp. 129–86; *The Fount of Chemical Truth,* in *HM,* II, 261.
11. Read, p. 137.
12. Philalethes, *The Metamorphosis of Metals,* in *HM,* II, 228–29.
13. Kelly, p. 13.
14. John Frederick Helvetius, *Golden Calf,* in *HM,* II, 278.
15. Lacinius, p. 46.
16. E. J. Holmyard, *Alchemy* (Harmondsworth, Middlesex: Penguin Books, 1957), p. 196. Roland McHugh, "Recipis for the Price of the Coffin," in *A Conceptual Guide,* pp. 23–24, also notes the importance of John Foster's Corn Law of 1784 in "fostering wheat crops."
17. Ripley, *Compound,* in *TCB,* p. 148.
18. Lacinius, pp. 414–15.
19. Ripley, *Compound,* in *TCB,* p. 148.
20. *Compound,* in *TCB,* p. 176.
21. Read, p. 139.
22. In *HM,* II, 261.
23. H. M. E. DeJong, *Michael Maier's Atalanta Fugiens* (Leiden: E. J. Brill, 1969), pp. 132–33. See Emblem XIV, p. 390 for an illustration of the ouroboros.
24. "Circling the Square," in *A James Joyce Miscellany III,* ed. Marvin Magalaner (Carbondale: Southern Illinois University Press, 1962), p. 240.

25. *An Open Entrance to the Closed Palace of the King,* in *HM,* II, 201–23; *The Sophic Hydrolith,* in *HM,* I, 83; frontispiece to *HM,* I, II.

26. Nicholas Flamell, *A Short Tract, or Philosophical Summary,* in *HM,* I, 142.

27. Paracelsus quoted by Helvetius in *The Golden Calf,* in *HM,* II, 278–79.

28. Quoted in Helvetius, *The Golden Calf,* in *HM,* II, 279.

29. *Third Census,* p. xlviii.

30. Trismosin, quoting from the *Turba Philosophorum,* p. 74.

31. Read, p. 14.

32. Campbell and Robinson, p. 184n.

33. Philalethes, *The Fount of Chemical Truth,* in *HM,* II, 265.

34. *An Open Entrance,* in *HM,* II, 178.

35. *The New Chemical Light Drawn from the Fountain of Nature and of Manual Experience,* in *HM,* II, 136.

36. J. K., trans., Theophrastus Paracelsus, *The Prophecies of Paracelsus* (London: William Rider & Son, 1915), pp. 32–33, 42.

37. *Sophic Hydrolith,* in *HM,* I, 82. See also *The Glory of the World,* in *HM,* I, 183; and Flamell, *A Short Tract,* in *HM,* I, 146, where the result of the process is a chicken "that will deliver you with its blood from all diseases, and feed you with its flesh, and clothe you with its feathers, and shelter you from the cold." Garvin associates the hen with Madame Blavatsky (p. 305), while Troy thinks she is a form of Isis (p. 42). Hugh Kenner, *Dublin's Joyce* (Bloomington: Indiana University Press, 1956), pp. 306–08, finds only voices, words, and rhetorical devices in this passage.

38. Kenner, p. 343.

39. Arthur Edward Waite, *Lives of Alchemystical Philosophers* (London: George Ridway, 1888), p. 164. For a complete exploration of Boehme in Joyce's works, see Sister Generose Gabel, "James Joyce, Jacob Boehme, and the Mystic Way," Diss. University of Wisconsin-Madison 1977.

40. Ian MacArthur, "Alchemical Elements of *Finnegans Wake,*" *A Wake Newslitter,* 12 (1975), 20.

41. Hart, p. 102.

42. *Fount,* in *HM,* II, 261.

43. Philalethes, *Fount,* in *HM,* II, 261–62.

44. *Compound,* in *TCB,* p. 172.

45. The term is Campbell and Robinson's, p. 276.

Number Symbolism

1. Jung, *Psychology and Alchemy,* p. 23.
2. *Psychology of the Transference,* p. 45.
3. *Compound,* in *TCB,* between pp. 106–07.
4. *HM,* I, 4.
5. Sendivogius, *The New Chemical Light,* in *HM,* II, 142–43.
6. Quoted in *The Golden Tract,* in *HM,* I, 14.
7. *Psychology and Alchemy,* pp. 26–27.
8. Campbell and Robinson, p. 45n.
9. *The Sigla of "Finnegans Wake"* (London: Edward Arnold, 1976), pp. 96–99.
10. In *HM,* I, 73.
11. MacArthur, p. 21.
12. *Eternal Geomater* (Carbondale and Edwardsville: Southern Illinois University Press, 1969), pp. 40, 42–48, 14.
13. Hart, p. 63.
14. MacArthur, p. 20.
15. Hart, pp. 62–63.
16. Michaelis Meyeri, *Viridarium Chymicum* (Frankfurt: n.p., 1688), pp. 21, 77.
17. Sendivogius, *The New Chemical Light,* in *HM,* II, 143.
18. In *HM,* I, 14, 9.
19. *The Glory of the World,* in *HM,* I, 178.
20. Jung, *Psychology of the Transference,* p. 5.
21. *Psychology and Alchemy,* pp. 329–30. *Atalanta Fugiens* contains many references to incest; see DeJong, Emblem IV, p. 280, explanation, pp. 191–95.
22. In *HM,* I, 46–50.
23. *Psychology of the Transference,* p. 53.
24. *Psychology of the Transference,* p. 101.
25. *Mysterium Coniunctionis,* Vol. XIV of *The Collected Works of C. G. Jung,* trans. R. F. C. Hull, 2nd ed., Bollingen Series XX (Princeton: Princeton University Press, 1970), pp. 90–91.
26. Jung, *Psychology and Alchemy,* p. 237.
27. Ripley, *Compound,* in *TCB,* pp. 146, 147; Gerard Heym, "Some Alchemical Picture Books," *Ambix,* 1 (1937), 74.
28. A. E. Waite, "Woman and the Hermetic Mystery," *The Occult*

Review, 15 (1912), 325–26, quoted in H. Stanley Redgrove, *Bygone Beliefs* (London: Rider & Son, 1920), pp. 178–79.

29. Yeats, "Rosa Alchemica," p. 484.

30. Yeats, "Rosa Alchemica," p. 477.

31. John Maxson Stillman, *Theophrastus Bombastus Von Hohenheim Called Paracelsus* (London: Open Court Publishing Co., 1920), p. 65.

32. Atherton, p. 250.

33. MacArthur, p. 20.

34. Hart, pp. 129–30.

35. MacArthur, p. 21.

36. McHugh, p. 72.

37. MacArthur, p. 21.

38. Jung, *Psychology and Alchemy*, pp. 412–13. There are, of course, other possible sources for the incest motif in *Finnegans Wake* besides alchemy. J. Mitchell Morse, *The Sympathetic Alien* (N.Y.: New York University Press, 1959), p. 42, discusses "Erigena's doctrine that Eve was in every sense a part of Adam's self, with which he yearned to be reunited. Earwicker's secret lust for his daughter is more than merely incestuous, for she is also his wife, as Eve was Adam's daughter. On this view, all sexual relationships are essentially narcissistic and there is no such thing as complete or genuine heterosexuality." Fritz Senn, "Insects Appalling," in *Twelve and a Tilly*, ed. Jack P. Dalton and Clive Hart (London: Faber & Faber, 1966), pp. 36–39, relates the incest motif to the insects with which the *Wake* teems. Hugh Kenner, *Dublin's Joyce*, p. 288, ties it to Dodgson's affections for Alice Liddell and Isa Bowman. In *Ulysses* Stephen Dedalus points out that the psychoanalysts were not the first to speculate on the origin of incest: "—Saint Thomas, Stephen, smiling, said, whose gorbellied works I enjoy reading in the original, writing of incest from a standpoint different from that of the new Viennese school Mr Magee spoke of, likens it in his wise and curious way to an avarice of the emotions." (*U* 205)

39. *Practica, or Twelve Keys*, in *HM*, I, 352, 348–49.

40. Campbell and Robinson, pp. 165–66.

41. MacArthur, p. 21.

42. Petr Beckmann, *A History of* π *(Pi)*, 2nd ed. (Boulder, Colo.: Golem Press, 1971), pp. 39–41, 46–49, 169–78.

43. Beckmann, pp. 163–65; Benjamin Bold, *Famous Problems of Mathematics* (N.Y.: Van Nostrand Reinhold, 1969), pp. 47–48.

44. Robert Boyle, S.J., pointed out Dante's use of this image at the Seventh International James Joyce Symposium, Zurich, June 1979.

45. Noted by MacArthur, p. 19.

46. DeJong, p. 166 (Emblem XXI, p. 397).

47. Ripley, *Compound,* in *TCB,* p. 112.

48. Kenner, pp. 327–28. For other interpretations of and sources for the diagram, see Boldereff, pp. 113–38; McHugh, pp. 67–76.

49. *Psychology of the Transference,* p. 42.

50. "The Porters: A Square Performance of Three Tiers in the Round," in *A Conceptual Guide,* p. 203.

51. *Integration of the Personality,* p. 227.

52. Norris, pp. 139–40.

53. McHugh, p. 121.

54. Hart, p. 77.

55. Tindall, *A Reader's Guide,* p. 116.

56. Hart, pp. 62, 102.

57. Trismosin, p. 32.

Colors and Forgery

1. Ross, "Alchemy," 11th *Encyclopedia Britannica,* I, 519.

2. "Originality and Repetition in *Finnegans Wake* and *Ulysses,*" *PMLA,* 94 (1979), 109.

3. *The Golden Tripod,* in *HM,* I, 345.

4. *Psychology and Alchemy,* p. 187.

5. *Philosophia Reformata,* quoted in Read, p. 271.

6. "The Opening Paragraphs (Contd.)," *A Wake Newslitter,* 2 (1965), 19.

7. *Bloomefields Blossoms,* in *TCB,* p. 321.

8. *Reader's Guide,* p. 321.

9. *Ordinall,* in *TCB,* pp. 64–66.

10. Ernst von Meyer, *A History of Chemistry from Earliest Times to the Present Day,* trans. George McGowan, 3rd Eng. ed., trans. from 3rd German ed. (London: Macmillan, 1906), p. 41.

11. Lacinius, pp. 68–69.

12. Meyer, pp. 40–41.

13. Harry Levin, *James Joyce* (New York: New Directions, 1941), pp. 178–79.

14. Norris, p. 91.

15. "Rosa Alchemica," p. 466.

16. *An Open Entrance,* in *HM,* II, 167.

17. Hart, pp. 111, 203.

18. Atherton, p. 67.

19. John Maxson Stillman, *The Story of Alchemy and Early Chemistry,* originally published in 1924 as *The Story of Early Chemistry* (N.Y.: Dover Publications, 1960), p. 375.

20. Stillman, *Theophrastus,* pp. 39–46. See also Stillman, *Story of Alchemy,* pp. 372–77.

21. *Ordinall,* in *TCB,* p. 25.

22. J. K., Explanatory Notes, *Splendor Solis,* p. 90.

23. Trismosin, p. 88.

24. J. K., Explanatory Notes, *Splendor Solis,* pp. 95, 103–04.

25. Joyce to Frank Budgen (dictated), quoted in Glasheen, *Third Census,* p. lxviii.

26. "Saint Patrick in *FW,*" *A Wake Newslitter,* 4 (1967), p. 88; "The Quoniam Page from the Book of Kells," *A Wake Newslitter,* 11 (1974), p. 86; Atherton, p. 47. For other interpretations of this passage, see Hodgart, p. 185; Norris, pp. 88–91; Michael Begnal, "The Dreamers at the Wake: A View of Narration and Point of View," in *Narrator and Character in "Finnegans Wake"* (Lewisburg: Bucknell University Press, 1975), pp. 106–08.

27. *Reader's Guide,* p. 320.

28. *The Life of St. Patrick and His Place in History* (N.Y.: Macmillan, 1905), pp. 109–10.

29. *New Chemical Light,* in *HM,* II, 93.

30. Hayman, *A First-Draft Version of "Finnegans Wake,"* p. 279.

31. *New Chemical Light,* in *HM,* II, 94.

32. *New Chemical Light,* in *HM,* II, 94.

33. *New Chemical Light,* in *HM,* II, 100–02.

34. *New Chemical Light,* in *HM,* II, 101.

35. *New Chemical Light,* in *HM,* II, 102.

36. *Reader's Guide,* p. 319. Michael H. Begnal, "The Dreamers at the Wake," pp. 106–09 also identifies Berkeley with Shem. Glasheen, however, identifies Patrick with Shem, *Third Census,* p. lxix.

37. *New Chemical Light,* in *HM,* II, 82.

38. Begnal claims that "Shem may be defeated in fact, but he is the

victor in spirit," "The Dreamers at the Wake," p. 108. He bases this on the fact that, "Rather than gazing at the ground in submission, Shem is the character who turns his eyes to the heavens." Begnal is mistaken, however, in asserting that those who look toward the heavens and spurn the earth are the victors in *Finnegans Wake;* all of the alchemical allusions emphasize the need for both the earth and the heavens.

Ingredients and Equipment

1. C. G. Jung, *Alchemical Studies,* Vol. XIII of *The Collected Works of C. G. Jung,* trans. R. F. C. Hull, Bollingen Series XX (Princeton: Princeton University Press, 1967), p. 235.

2. Stillman, *Story of Alchemy,* p. 20.

3. Read, pp. 40–41; Chaucer, 1. 790, p. 216; Read, p. 309n.20.

4. Waite, *Lives of Alchemystical Philosophers,* p. 139.

5. Helene Petrovna Blavatsky, *Iris Unveiled* (1877; rpt. Pasadena, Calif.: Theosophical University Press, 1960), I, 191.

6. Stillman, *Theophrastus,* p. 160.

7. Arthur John Hopkins, *Alchemy* (N.Y.: AMS Press, 1967), pp. 116–17.

8. MacArthur, p. 21. For the alchemical uses of arsenic and bismuth, see Read, p. 49; Stillman, *Story of Alchemy,* p. 314.

9. Ross, "Alchemy," 11th *Encyclopedia Britannica,* I, 520. In *Rosarium Philosophorum* (Frankfurt: n.p., 1550), illustrations depicting the process as the union of King and Queen show these two figures associated with the sun and moon, respectively.

10. MacArthur, p. 20.

11. The identification of these references to Glauber's work is MacArthur's, p. 20.

12. The term is Campbell and Robinson's, p. 279.

13. MacArthur, pp. 22–23; Read, pp. 132–33.

14. *Story of Alchemy,* p. 68.

15. Read, pp. 120–21.

16. "Woman and the Hermetic Mystery," p. 325, quoted in Redgrove, *Bygone Beliefs,* p. 177; Joseph Campbell, *The Masks of God: Creative Mythology* (N.Y.: Viking, 1968), p. 267.

17. Norton, *Ordinall,* in *TCB,* p. 41.

18. Jung, *Alchemical Studies,* pp. 131–32n.

19. Read, p. 155.
20. MacArthur, p. 23.
21. Arthur and Elizabeth Rose, *The Condensed Chemical Dictionary,* 7th ed. (N.Y.: Reinhold Publishing Corporation, 1966), p. 547.
22. Holmyard, p. 26.
23. Philalethes, *Fount,* in *HM,* II, 265.
24. Campbell and Robinson, p. 346n.
25. For other illustrations of the King's Bath, see *Rosarium Philosophorum,* illus. 3, n. pag.; Meyeri, *Viridarium Chymicum,* pp. 53–54, 90.

Shem the "Alshemist"

1. "*Finnegans Wake,* Page 185: An Explication," *James Joyce Quarterly,* 4 (1966), 3–16.
2. Ripley, *Compound,* in *TCB,* p. 153.
3. Read, pp. 37–38.
4. Ross, "Alchemy," 11th *Encyclopedia Britannica,* I, 520.
5. Here, as elsewhere in this study, I realize that the alchemical interpretations are not exclusive, nor always even the primary interpretations. "Scoppialamina" is certainly a reference to a drug taken by Joyce for his eye problems, and this whole phrase is definitely medical, as J. B. Lyons points out in *Joyce* & *Medicine* (Dublin: Dolmen Press, 1973), pp. 183, 206–07. However, I have deliberately restricted myself to alchemical allusions for the sake of brevity and coherence.
6. *Sophic Hydrolith,* in *HM,* I, 102. The importance of the number forty in the alchemical process is also emphasized by Edward Kelly in "The Humid Path," *The Alchemical Writings,* pp. 100, 105.
7. Holmyard, p. 65.
8. Holmyard, p. 26.
9. Holmyard, p. 44. Many alchemists were concerned with the degree of fire applied in the process of transmutation and caution strongly against using too hot a fire. See, for example, *An Open Entrance,* in *HM,* II, pp. 188–89.
10. *Ordinall,* in *TCB,* p. 90.
11. *Compound,* in *TCB,* p. 186.

12. Quoted in Stillman, *Story of Alchemy,* p. 179.

13. Stillman, *Story of Alchemy,* p. 180.

14. *Ordinall,* in *TCB,* pp. 41, 42.

15. *Open Entrance,* in *HM,* II, 183–84; *Bloomefields Blossoms,* in *TCB,* p. 321.

16. Holmyard, p. 47.

17. Lévi, p. 223.

18. Reference noted by MacArthur, p. 20.

19. *The Triumphal Chariot of Antimony* ([England]: n.p., 1660), pp. 78, 93, 115, 121.

20. "Rosa Alchemica," p. 484.

21. Quoted in Campbell, *Creative Mythology,* pp. 263–64.

22. *Ordinall,* in *TCB,* p. 11.

23. C. G. Jung, *Symbols of Transformation,* Vol. V of *The Collected Works of C. G. Jung,* trans. R. F. C. Hull, 2nd ed., Bollingen Series XX (Princeton: Princeton University Press, 1967), p. 189.

24. *The Psychology of the Transference,* p. 25. This is a common theme of alchemy—that the goal, although found in the vilest of substances, is the most precious.

25. *Life Against Death* (Middletown, Conn.: Wesleyan University Press, 1959), p. 194.

26. "*Finnegans Wake,* Page 185," p. 11.

27. *Creative Mythology,* pp. 272–73.

28. *Sophic Hydrolith,* in *HM,* I, 93. The comparison continues for several pages.

Bibliography

I. Works Related to Joyce and Finnegans Wake

Atherton, James S. *The Books at the Wake: A Study of Literary Allusions in James Joyce's "Finnegans Wake."* N.Y.: Viking Press, 1960.

Beckett, Samuel, et. al. *Our Exagmination Round His Factification for Incamination of Work in Progress.* 2nd ed. Northampton: John Dickens & Conner, 1962.

Beckmann, Petr. *A History of π (Pi).* 2nd ed. Boulder, Colo.: Golem Press, 1971.

Begnal, Michael H., and Grace Eckley. *Narrator and Character in "Finnegans Wake."* Lewisburg: Bucknell University Press, 1975.

———, and Fritz Senn, eds. *A Conceptual Guide to "Finnegans Wake."* University Park: Penn. State University Press, 1974.

Benstock, Bernard. *Joyce-Again's Wake: An Analysis of "Finnegans Wake."* Seattle: University of Washington Press, 1965.

Bold, Benjamin. *Famous Problems of Mathematics: A History of Constructions with Straight Edge and Compasses.* N.Y.: Van Nostrand Reinhold, 1969.

Boldereff, Frances Motz. *Hermes to His Son Thoth: Being Joyce's Use of Giordano Bruno in "Finnegans Wake."* Woodward, Pa.: Classic Nonfiction Library, 1968.

———. *Reading "Finnegans Wake."* Woodward, Pa.: Classic Nonfiction Library, 1959.

Bonheim, Helmut. *Joyce's Benefictions.* Berkeley: University of California Press, 1964.

Bowen, Zack. *Musical Allusions in the Works of James Joyce: Early Poetry Through "Ulysses."* Albany: State University of New York Press, 1974.

Boyle, Robert, S. J. "*Finnegans Wake,* Page 185: An Explication." *James Joyce Quarterly,* 4 (1966), 3–16.

———. "*Finnegans Wake*: The Artist as Coprophiliac." Lecture, SUNY Binghamton. 15 April 1972.

———. *James Joyce's Pauline Vision: A Catholic Exposition.* Carbondale and Edwardsville: Southern Illinois University Press, 1978.

———. "Miracle in Black Ink: A Glance at Joyce's Use of His Eucharistic Image." *James Joyce Quarterly,* 10 (1972), 47–60.

Broes, Arthur T. "More People at the Wake (Contd.)." *A Wake Newslitter,* 4 (1967), 25–30.

Brown, Norman O. *Life Against Death: The Psychoanalytic Meaning of History.* Middletown, Conn.: Wesleyan University Press, 1959.

Bury, J. B. *The Life of St. Patrick and His Place in History.* N.Y.: Macmillan, 1905.

Campbell, Joseph. *The Masks of God: Creative Mythology.* N.Y.: Viking Press, 1968.

———, and Henry Morton Robinson. *A Skeleton Key to "Finnegans Wake."* 1944; rpt. N.Y.: Viking Press, 1966.

Carver, Craig. "James Joyce and the Theory of Magic." *James Joyce Quarterly,* 15 (1978), 201–14.

Cixous, Hélène. *The Exile of James Joyce.* Trans. Sally A. J. Purcell. N.Y.: David Lewis, 1972.

Connolly, Thomas E. *The Personal Library of James Joyce: A Descriptive Bibliography.* University of Buffalo Studies, 22 (1955), 5–58.

———, ed. *Scribbledehobble: The Ur-Workbook for "Finnegans Wake."* Evanston, Ill.: Northwestern University Press, 1961.

Dalton, Jack P., and Clive Hart, eds. *Twelve and a Tilly: Essays on the Occasion of the 25th Anniversary of "Finnegans Wake."* London: Faber & Faber, 1966.

Dante Alighieri. *Paradiso.* Vol. III of *The Divine Comedy.* Trans., with a commentary by Charles S. Singleton. Bollingen Series LXXX. Princeton: Princeton University Press, 1975.

Ellmann, Richard. *The Consciousness of James Joyce.* London: Faber & Faber, 1977.

———. *James Joyce.* N.Y.: Oxford University Press, 1959.

Gabel, C. S. A., Sister Generose. "James Joyce, Jacob Boehme, and the Mystic Way." *DAI,* Ser. A, 38 (1978), 7323A (University of Wisconsin-Madison).

Garvin, John. *James Joyce's Disunited Kingdom and the Irish Dimension*. Dublin: Gill and MacMillan, 1976.

Gilbert, Stuart. *James Joyce's "Ulysses."* Vintage Books, 1955.

Givens, Sean, ed. *James Joyce: Two Decades of Criticism*. N.Y.: Vanguard Press, 1948.

Glasheen, Adaline. "The Opening Paragraphs (Contd.)." *A Wake Newslitter*, 2 (1965), 17–22.

———. *Third Census of "Finnegans Wake": An Index of the Characters and Their Roles*. Berkeley: University of California Press, 1977.

Golden, Séan. "The Quoniam Page from the Book of Kells." *A Wake Newslitter*, 11 (1974), 85–86.

Harkness, Marguerite. "Esthetics of Dedalus and Bloom: Nineteenth Century Roots, Structural Metaphors, and Resolutions." Diss. State University of New York at Binghamton 1974.

Hart, Clive. *A Concordance to "Finnegans Wake."* Minneapolis: University of Minnesota Press, 1963.

———. *Structure and Motif in "Finnegans Wake."* London: Faber & Faber, 1962.

———, and Fritz Senn, eds. *A Wake Digest*. Sydney: Sydney University Press, 1968.

Hayman, David, ed. *A First-Draft Version of "Finnegans Wake."* Austin: University of Texas Press, 1963.

Hodgart, Matthew. *James Joyce: A Student's Guide*. London: Routledge & Kegan Paul, 1978.

In the Wake of the "Wake." Tri-Quarterly, 38 (1977).

Joyce, James. *The Critical Writings*. Ed. Ellsworth Mason and Richard Ellmann. N.Y.: Viking Press, 1972.

———. MS ADD 47471b, 47474, 47475, 47476a, 47476b. *Finnegans Wake* Manuscripts. British Library, London, England.

Joyce, Stanislaus. *My Brother's Keeper: James Joyce's Early Years*. Ed. with an intro. and notes by Richard Ellmann. Preface by T. S. Eliot. N.Y.: Viking Press, 1969.

Kenner, Hugh. *Dublin's Joyce*. Bloomington: Indiana University Press, 1956.

———. *Joyce's Voices*. Berkeley: University of California Press, 1978.

Koch, Ronald J. "Giordano Bruno and *Finnegans Wake*." *James Joyce Quarterly*, 9 (1971), 225–49.

Kopper, Edward A. "Saint Patrick in *FW*." *A Wake Newslitter*, 4 (1967), 85–93.

Levin, Harry. *James Joyce: A Critical Introduction.* N.Y.: New Directions, 1941.

Levine, Jennifer Schiffer. "Originality and Repetition in *Finnegans Wake* and *Ulysses.*" *PMLA*, 94 (1979), 106–120.

Litz, A. Walton. *The Art of James Joyce: Method and Design in "Ulysses" and "Finnegans Wake."* N.Y.: Oxford University Press, 1961.

Lyons, J. B. *James Joyce and Medicine.* Dublin: Dolmen Press, 1973.

MacArthur, Ian. "Alchemical Elements of *Finnegans Wake.*" *A Wake Newslitter,* 12 (1975), 19–23.

McHugh, Roland. *The Sigla of "Finnegans Wake."* London: Edward Arnold, 1976.

Magalaner, Marvin, ed. *A James Joyce Miscellany, III.* Carbondale: Southern Illinois University Press, 1962.

Morse, J. Mitchell. *The Sympathetic Alien: James Joyce and Catholicism.* N.Y.: N.Y. University Press, 1959.

Norris, Margot. *The Decentered Universe of "Finnegans Wake": A Structuralist Analysis.* Baltimore: Johns Hopkins University Press, 1974.

O'Brien, Darcy. *The Conscience of James Joyce.* Princeton: Princeton University Press, 1968.

Solomon, Margaret C. *Eternal Geomater: The Sexual Universe of "Finnegans Wake."* Carbondale and Edwardsville: Southern Illinois University Press, 1969.

———. "Sham Rocks: Shem's Answer to the First Riddle of the Universe." *A Wake Newslitter,* 7 (1970), 67–72.

Tindall, William York. "James Joyce and the Hermetic Tradition." *Journal of the History of Ideas,* 15 (1954), 23–39.

———. *A Reader's Guide to "Finnegans Wake."* N.Y.: Farrar, Straus & Giroux, 1969.

Troy, Mark L. *Mummeries of Resurrection: The Cycle of Osiris in "Finnegans Wake."* Uppsala: University of Uppsala, 1976.

Von Phul, Ruth. "Mummer in Motley." Lecture, SUNY Binghamton. 24 April 1972.

Yeats, William Butler. "Rosa Alchemica." In *Early Poems and Stories.* London: Macmillan, 1925.

II. Works Related to Alchemy

Ashmole, Elias, ed. *Theatrum Chemicum Britannicum: Containing Severall Poeticall Pieces of our Famous English Philosophers, who have written the Hermetique Mysteries in their owne Ancient Language*. The Sources of Science, no. 39. 1652; rpt. London: Johnson Reprint Corporation, 1967.

Atwood, M. A. *Hermetic Philosophy and Alchemy: A Suggestive Inquiry into "THE HERMETIC MYSTERY."* Revised ed., with intro. by Walter Leslie Wilmhurst. Re-issue of text published anonymously in 1850 under the title *The Suggestive Inquiry Into the Hermetic Mystery*. N.Y.: Julian Press, 1960.

Blavatsky, Helene Petrovna. *Isis Unveiled: A Master-Key to the Mysteries of Ancient and Modern Science and Theology*. 2 vols. 1877; rpt. Pasadena, Calif.: Theosophical University Press, 1960.

DeJong, H. M. E. *Michael Maier's Atalanta Fugiens: Sources of an Alchemical Book of Emblems*. Leiden: E. J. Brill, 1969.

Federman, Reinhard. *The Royal Art of Alchemy*. Trans. Richard H. Weber. N.Y.: Chilton Book Co., 1964.

Griffith, Francis Llewellyn. "Hermes Trismegistus." *Encyclopedia Britannica*. 11th ed. (1910–11).

———. "Thoth." *Encyclopedia Britannica*. 11th ed. (1910–11).

Heym, Gerard. "Some Alchemical Picture Books." *Ambix*, 1 (1937), 69–75.

Holmyard, E. J. *Alchemy*. Harmondsworth, Middlesex: Penguin Books, 1957.

Hopkins, Arthur John. *Alchemy: Child of Greek Philosophy*. Preface 1933. N.Y.: AMS Press, 1967.

Jung, C. G. *Alchemical Studies*. Vol. XIII of *The Collected Works of C. G. Jung*. Trans. R. F. C. Hull. Bollingen Series XX. Princeton: Princeton University Press, 1967.

———. *The Integration of the Personality*. Trans. Stanley Dell. London: Lowe & Brydone, 1940.

———. *Mysterium Coniunctionis*. Vol. XIV of *The Collected Works of C. G. Jung*. Trans R. F. C. Hull. Bollingen Series XX. 2nd ed. Princeton University Press, 1970.

———. *Psychology and Alchemy*. Vol. XII of *The Collected Works of C. G. Jung*. Trans. R. F. C. Hull. Bollingen Series XX. 2nd ed. Princeton: Princeton University Press, 1968.

———. *The Psychology of the Transference*. Trans. R. F. C. Hull. Princeton: Princeton University Press, 1954.

———. *Symbols of Transformation: An Analysis of the Prelude to a Case of Schizophrenia*. Vol. V of *The Collected Works of C. G. Jung*. Trans. R. F. C. Hull. Bollingen Series XX. 2nd ed. N.Y.: Bollingen Foundation, 1967.

———. "Transformation Symbolism in the Mass." In *Psyche and Symbol: A Selection from the Writings of C. G. Jung*. Ed. Violet de Laszlo. Trans. R. F. C. Hull and Monica Curtis. Garden City, N.Y.: Doubleday, 1958, pp. 148–224.

Kelly, Edward. *The Alchemical Writings*. Trans., ed. with a biographical preface by A. E. Waite. Hamburg, 1676; rpt. London: James Elliott, 1893.

Lacinius, Janus. *The New Pearl of Great Price: A Treatise Concerning the Treasure and Most Precious Stone of the Philosophers*. The original Aldine edition translated into English. London: James Elliott, 1894.

Lévi, Éliphas (pseudonym of Alphonse Louis Constant). *Transcendental Magic: Its Doctrine and Ritual*. Trans., intro., annotated by A. E. Waite. 1896; rpt. London: Rider and Co., 1968.

Mead, G. R. S., ed. and trans. *Thrice-Greatest Hermes: Studies in Hellenistic Theosophy and Gnosis*. 3 vols. London: Theosophical Publishing Society, 1906.

Meyer, Ernst von. *A History of Chemistry from Earliest Times to the Present Day, Being Also an Introduction to the Science*. Trans. George McGowan. 3rd Eng. ed., trans. from the 3rd German ed., with various additions and alterations. London: Macmillan, 1906.

Meyeri, Michaelis. *Viridarium Chymicum*. Frankfurt: n.p., 1688.

Paracelsus, Theophrastus. *The Prophecies of Paracelsus: Magic Figures and Prognostications Made by Theophrastus Paracelsus About Four Hundred Years Ago*. Trans. and intro. by J. K. London: William Rider & Son, 1915.

"Paracelsus." *Encyclopedia Britannica*. 11th ed. (1910–11).

Read, John. *Prelude to Chemistry: An Outline of Alchemy, its Literature and Relationships*. London, 1936; rpt. Cambridge, Mass.: M.I.T. Press, 1966.

Redgrove, H. Stanley. *Alchemy: Ancient and Modern*. 2nd ed., rev. London: William Rider & Son, 1922.

———. *Bygone Beliefs: Being a Series of Excursions in the Byways of Thought*. London: William Rider & Son, 1920.

Rosarium Philosophorum. Frankfurt: n.p., 1550.

Rose, Arthur, and Elizabeth Rose. *The Condensed Chemical Dictionary*. 7th ed., rev. and enlarged. N.Y.: Reinhold, 1966.

Ross, Hugh Munro. "Alchemy." *Encyclopedia Britannica*. 11th ed. (1910–11).

Sheppard, H. J. "The Ouroboros and the Unity of Matter in Alchemy; A Study in Origins." *Ambix*, 10 (1962), 83–96.

Stillman, John Maxson. *The Story of Alchemy and Early Chemistry.* Originally published 1924 as *The Story of Early Chemistry.* N.Y.: Dover Publications, 1960.

———. *Theophrastus Bombastus Von Hohenheim Called Paracelsus: His Personality and Influence as Physician, Chemist and Reformer.* London: Open Court Publishing Co., 1920.

Swainson, W. P. *Theophrastus Paracelsus: Mediaeval Alchemist.* London: William Rider & Son, 1919.

Taylor, F. Sherwood. *The Alchemists: Founders of Modern Chemistry.* 1949; rpt. N.Y.: Arno Press, 1974.

Trismosin, Solomon. *Splendor Solis.* Explanatory notes by J. K. London: Kegan Paul, Trench, Trubner & Co., [1920].

Valentine, Basil. *The Triumphal Chariot of Antimony.* [England]: n.p., 1660.

Waite, Arthur Edward, ed. *The Hermetic Museum, Restored and Enlarged.* 2 vols. London: James Elliott, 1893.

———. *Lives of Alchemystical Philosophers.* London: George Ridway, 1888.

Index